DIAGNOSING TOXIC LEADERSHIP

DIAGNOSING T☢XIC LEADERSHIP

Understanding the Connection Between
Personality Disorders and Toxic Leader Behaviors

BASED ON ACTUAL CASE STUDIES

DR. OLLIE G. BARNES III

For information about this title contact the publisher:

Impact Publishing Company
7119 Winter Forest Dr.
Portage Michigan 49024

ISBNs:
979-8-9900035-0-7 (hardcover)
979-8-9900035-1-4 (softcover)
979-8-9900035-2-1 (eBook)

Printed in the United States of America

Cover and Interior design: Collaboration between 1106 Design and Impact Publishing

This book is dedicated to Jesus Christ the foundation of my life, my loving parents Ollie Jr. and Marlene Barnes, My Grand Parents, Ollie Sr. and Thelma Barnes and Ruth Dogan. My loving and supportive best friend and wife Dr. Toni Yvette Woolfork-Barnes and our son the "Morehouse Man" Ollie G. Barnes IV. My Sibling Cynthea Lester and Kenny Barnes.

Table of Contents

Foreword ix

Preface xi

SECTION I: The Narcissistic Leader 1

SECTION II: The Passive-Aggressive Leader 31

SECTION III: Borderline Personality Disorder 57

SECTION IV: Organizational Impact 85

SECTION V: Diagnostic Techniques, Clinical Insights,
and Consulting Practice 105

SECTION VI: The Future of Work 149

Sources 179

Acknowledgments 183

About the Author 187

Index 189

Foreword

Larry D. Irey, Ph.D.
Clinical Psychologist

This is really good stuff. I like how you've taken the more clinical symptoms and patterns of personality disorders and translated them into specific patterns of behavior that toxic leaders display in the workplace. The details, specifics, and examples of these patterns make them very recognizable in a work setting. While the clinical basis for your insights is clear, the descriptions of actions and behavior patterns in non-clinical terms are excellently done. I am not sure I could have made that translation in such clear and applicable ways for those in the workplace. Your experience in dealing with personality disorders in leaders, along with your clinical training and consulting experience, brings a depth that isn't always present in business writings. I also think the emphasis on looking beyond the immediate level in the organization where the problems are displayed to assess leaders and processes at least one or two levels above is so important. This approach allows for accurate problem assessment and the creation of targeted solutions and interventions that have a real chance of being effective.

Preface

Toxic leaders poison the organizations they are selected by and entrusted to lead. Human-resource professionals, executive coaches, and organizational-development professionals are called to diagnose and repair poorly functioning organizational issues. The toxic leader's impact is often overlooked and minimized, especially when the leader holds a position of power or status, such as CEO, team leader, or even as pastor of a large religious community. The greater the leader's status and influence in their organization or community, the more sensitive the task of addressing the leader's behaviors. When the root cause of the problem is overlooked, talented employees will become frustrated and seek ways to exit the organization. They will transfer out of the department, leave the company, or in the worst-case scenario, stay in a dysfunctional system and become completely disengaged. The employee who chooses to stay learns to fly under the radar and contribute minimally. These underperforming employees may become valuable simply because they "know where the bodies are buried." Damaged leaders continue with their behavior because they have been rewarded for it in some way in the past. This means the organization is now intentionally or unintentionally an enabler of the toxic leader's behavior and the culture they have created.

These long-term employees know the "secret code" of getting things done in the organization. This obscure knowledge is sometimes referred to as *institutional wisdom*. Employees won't share information because they know their value as an employee is functioning in the dysfunctional system and remaining loyal to the narcissistic leader, which also makes them enablers of the toxic behavior even if it is not happening directly to them.

The organization suffers when people do not contribute to their maximum potential. It costs employers 33 percent of a worker's annual salary to hire a replacement when employees leave, creating a material impact on the organization's bottom line. The organization will also face reputation risk, making it difficult to attract new hires. It's important to remember that people share information freely through social media these days.

Unfortunately, toxic leaders are often able to disguise the damage they are inflicting on the organization, even placing the blame on others. Human-resources professionals may begin to evaluate direct reports, teams, and organizational structure, spending months or years trying to identify the source of the problem while the toxic leader deflects any responsibility.

The delicate process of assessing the senior leader's behaviors must also be evaluated while assessing organizational strengths. This book explains how to recognize and diagnose the various toxic-leadership behaviors that stem from the most common personality disorders, including narcissistic personality disorder, borderline personality disorder, and passive-aggressive personality disorder.

The organization typically invests in keeping a toxic leader, erroneously perceiving that the leader's value would be difficult to replicate. As a result, they unknowingly build systems that keep and sustain the damaged leader while simultaneously creating a self-destructive system.

Preface

The behavior of the pernicious leader is often minimized, tolerated, and avoided. This creates enabling behaviors on the part of the organization. Meanwhile, visible and invisible fault lines emerge inside and outside of the organization. Turnover is an obvious consequence; however, the employees also endure a physical and psychological toll. The emotional stress manifests in physical symptoms such as chronic headaches, back pain, gastric discomfort, and inability to sleep nights before going into work. Employees operating on minimal sleep continually find themselves on edge, wondering what the unpredictable leader will do next. This level of emotional distress can also lead to "spillover" in the home, causing difficulty in family and marital relationships. Acute stress is known to produce illness, including heart disease, obesity, and several types of cancer. Insurance costs and absentee rates rise as employees develop severe illnesses.

Employees will not challenge the narcissistic leader. They tiptoe around the leader, waiting for direction. When direction does come, it's inconsistent from day to day, which adds to the employees' state of confusion. They will suffer in isolation, blaming themselves for not being able to produce.

This book will share examples of extreme toxic behavior from leaders in different industries and the techniques for creating effective organizational interventions to detoxify these unhealthy organizations. We will also look at the connection of toxic-leader behaviors to diagnosable personality disorders. We will discuss how these personality disorders can be a precursor of ineffective leadership styles that can derail the careers of exceptionally talented professionals. Learning and implementing these invaluable skills will increase operational efficiency and profitability and reduce organizational reputation risk.

The book contains several case studies based on a summary of actual experiences that will help the reader identify toxic behaviors while demonstrating solutions. I'm here to tell you that there is hope, and there is help. Organizations *can* flourish and achieve the vision of their purpose. Employees can thrive and contribute as they wish to, and the toxic leader will have the opportunity to remediate their own detrimental behaviors. The leader's great strengths have helped them achieve their status. Unfortunately, at times, these strengths have been developed while overlooking venomous behaviors that may be linked to personality traits. This book will help you identify how you and others in similar roles can intervene and help.

The Narcissistic Leader

Case Study 1.1

SALLY JANSSEN, the chief human resources officer (CHRO) of Worldwide Innovative Solutions, sat silently at her desk. She'd just finished talking to a manager of a high-potential (HiPo) colleague who had just quit, accepting a lateral position with one of the company's competitors. Sally was also startled to learn that Toni, a talented employee, had accepted this lateral position for less money. Unfortunately, the story was beginning to sound familiar, as other high-performing employees were fleeing the unit led by the notorious Robb Lockett in what seemed to be a mass exodus. Every professional who had left the recently restructured global commercial marketing (GCM) unit had complained about Robb. Sally cringed, noting that this was the fifth high-potential marketing senior director to leave the organization for a lateral or lower-paying position in the last eight months. The CEO was on high alert, as one of the exiting HiPo's sent a letter to the board of directors expressing his dissatisfaction and pointing out what he thought was wrong with Robb Lockett and the organization. The CEO was genuinely concerned because GCM was responsible for three of the company's largest brands, totaling a combined 63 percent of the company's revenue and equaling $28.1 billion. Robb's division had performed exceptionally well over the past eighteen months, and the board was elated with the impact on the company's financial performance. Rumors swirled around the company that Robb was on the board's short list to be the company's next CEO.

Several employees had reported examples of Robb's odd behavior to human resources and the company's ombudsman.

Tim, a well-liked and valued employee, recently had had the unfortunate experience of sitting in Robb's chair. Tim was running late for a meeting and attempted to discreetly slide into the room, grabbing the first chair in the back of the room by the door, which happened to be the chair Robb liked to sit in. Robb had some peculiar superstition that this chair held all the power in the room. Tim knew that Robb often sat in the first chair, although since he was late, he thought the meeting had already started. When Robb came in even later and saw Tim in his chair, he gave him a steely stare.

Robb began the meeting, presenting a recent competitive analysis. He turned to Tim and said, "You must know all the answers, Tim. What do you think?" Tim had no idea what to do. He replied, "No, Robb, I was waiting to see the full report." Robb mocked Tim in a singsong voice, repeating his words to him: "I need to see the full report." Robb continued, "Is there anything else you need, Tim? Is your coffee okay? Or does a guy like you drink tea?" This was an inappropriate insult about Tim being in a same-sex relationship.

Tim and the rest of the employees sat in awkward silence, enduring the meeting until Robb was done. When he got to the last slide, Robb threw the hard copy of the deck on the conference room table and stormed out of the room. After a couple of minutes to get over the shock, Mary said, "Tim, you really blew it. You know Robb is crazy about his chair." Tim replied, "I wasn't sure what to do. I was late, and I wanted to help." She replied, "Yeah, Robb is not likely to forget this anytime soon."

Several employees reported that Robb mocked and belittled Tim during the meeting. It appeared that Robb perceived Tim was claiming a leadership role by ignoring the unwritten rule, disrespecting him, and claiming his chair. The employees further reported that it seemed Robb's rant was intended to remind everyone that he was the boss and that they shouldn't forget he had the power to run meetings. Sally also learned that Tim was a new father, and she wondered if that might explain why he was late.

SALLY MEETS WITH TIM

Disturbed by the reports, Sally called Tim into her office for a meeting. Tim showed up looking disheveled. Sally shook his hand and said, "Congratulations! I hear you are a new dad!" Tim beamed, "Yeah, a little boy." Then Sally asked, "Shouldn't you be on paternity leave?" Tim explained, "We adopted Lukas." Sally's brow wrinkled as she explained, "Adoptions are 100 percent covered in our employee benefit plan." Tim added, "I took two days, but my partner can stay at home. We have high goals on our team, and I want to make sure that I'm in the top 10 percent of performers. This job is important to me. I invested hundreds of thousands of dollars in my education. Working in global commercial marketing has been a long-term dream for me." Tim added with a bright smile, "Lukas will understand."

Sally took a minute to respond. It was important to her that Tim trusted her. She wanted to make sure she did all she could to make Tim feel comfortable. Unfortunately, HR was not a function that was viewed as a resource for problem-solving at World Innovative Solutions. Sally recognized that HR's primary role was making employment offers and administering exit packages. When things got hairy with difficult situations, the CEO bypassed HR and consulted legal counsel. Rather than find solutions, the company resorted to damage control.

Tim looked Sally in the eye and stated, "I don't want to be in the wake of the 'Lockett or Lose It' employees." Sally was aware of the phrase "Lockett or Lose It." It had been touted by past and present employees when describing Robb's management style. The catchy tagline meant you were either with Robb Lockett, complying with his erratic demands, or you weren't. If you weren't, you'd better be prepared to lose your job.

Startled, Tim blinked a few times, not sure what to do. Finally, speaking slowly, he replied, "I'm not sure what you mean." Sally sat straight up in her chair, put her elbows on her desk, leaned forward, and said, "Tim, let me be straight with you. You are a valued employee here. We care about you as a performer and as a family man. I want you to flourish at World Innovative Solutions. We want you to have a meaningful and productive career here."

Tim nervously stood up and said, "Thank you, Sally" as he darted out of the office.

ORGANIZATIONAL REPERCUSSIONS

After Tim left her office, Sally did some rough calculations of the hard dollar cost of the employee exodus. The running total was nearly a million dollars. Robb was responsible for $28 billion in revenue, so in comparison, the loss seemed insignificant. Sally knew, however, that there were much better uses for a million dollars than dismissing it as a cost of doing business with an unstable, toxic leader.

The marketing department is responsible for strategic listening at World Innovative Solutions. Strategic listening is a process where all comments and posts are evaluated on all social-media channels. It's used as a format to manage reputation risk, measure customer satisfaction, review competitors, and watch for product-development opportunities. The marketing department analyzes trends, watches for risks, and makes recommendations about what they've learned. One unfortunate example the marketing department reported to HR was that there were several scathing comments about the company from past *and current* employees.

The social media posts from past and current employees said things like, "great salary, a great steppingstone in your career, but watch out for Robb Lockett—no one lasts longer than 12 months," and "Keep your employment attorney on speed dial; contact me for a good one." The posters added the hashtag #LockettorLoseIt. Senior leaders didn't take much notice of the information, even though it was submitted and discussed in quarterly meetings. They would say things like, "No one believes what they read on the Internet" and move on to discuss what they thought were more pressing business matters. Or they would say, "Well, that's just Robb being Robb."

When approached about the turnover, Robb would say that he wanted "high performers" and couldn't have "slackers" on his team. He was aware of, and liked, his #LockettorLoseIt moniker. He boasted that employees who couldn't last under his leadership "didn't pass his test." He said the way he treated people was strategic, and leadership bought this argument. The company was growing, and cash flow was strong, so they accepted Robb's statements as a reasonable argument. After all, results are results.

The next time Tim was rushing to work, he got into a car accident. His car was totaled. Tim shattered the femur in his right leg, the largest bone in the body. Healing would require surgery, resetting the bone, inserting pins to mend the bone where it had been destroyed, extensive physical therapy, and a long-term stay in a rehabilitation center. He was lucky to be alive.

Sally learned that Tim was also suing World Innovative Solutions. His lawsuit detailed how he felt too "intimidated" to take his full benefits package and noted there was a history of abusive behavior by Robb Lockett. The legal document included examples of social-media posts including the hashtag #LockettorLoseIt, with lists of people who were willing to testify. The prosecutors were requesting electronic discovery, an expensive process which could take years and require additional technological investment to satisfy the requirement. World Innovative Solutions' lawyers were now involved. Sally was no longer allowed to communicate with Tim because of the pending litigation.

ADDRESSING ROBB LOCKETT

Sally was required to interview Robb Lockett about the situation for the company records. Because of Robb's arrogance, there was no way he would come to Sally; she had to go to meet with him. Sally arrived for their scheduled appointment on time, however, Robb's assistant, Mary, instructed her to wait in the reception area.

Robb flung his office door open fifteen minutes past their agreed-upon time and showed Sally the way into his immaculate office. His walls were filled with awards and plaques that reminded him—and everyone who entered his office—just how good he was at everything he did. As Sally entered Robb's spotless office, she noticed pictures of Robb everywhere: standing next to Fortune 100 executives, well-known sports figures, world leaders, and pop-culture celebrities. The most noticeable were photos, mounted on wooden plaques, of Robb pointing to the rising quarterly performance numbers.

Robb motioned Sally toward an intimate table set aside for visitors. She took her seat while Robb grabbed two mugs full of coffee from his deluxe coffee station, a one-of-a-kind hand-crafted station, made of cocobolo, a rare and exotic wood from trees that grow only in Central America. He placed two mugs on the table. Robb's mug was imprinted with "My Way or the Highway." Sally's mug was plain and smaller than Robb's.

Sally boldly stated, "This is real, Robb." Robb's face was expressionless. She went on to say, "We've lost millions in turnover, and someone has become seriously hurt." Robb didn't respond. They sat in silence. Sally went on, "The electronic discovery is going to take years, stagnate progress, and cost a fortune."

Robb finally spoke up, saying, "We need to bring in a team of consultants to analyze our continual growth, to ensure we can continue on this path." He then ordered, "Sally, put out an RFP (Request for Proposal), and make sure you get only the best firms with top teams. I don't want any junior people here. We are positioned for significant success, and we need to make sure they provide their professional opinions regarding what we can do to stay on the positive trajectory."

Sally tried to bring the conversation back to the issue of his toxic behavior by saying, "I would, but I'm steeped in lawyer meetings, and the hourly rates are racking up." Robb stood up and said, "It'll take them three years to figure it out. We have a business to run. We can't manage this company with men who act like a chick on the rag. Real men don't get upset by a little hard work. I guess Tim wouldn't get that; I think he's the wife in his marriage." Robb used air quotes when using the word *marriage*, referring to Tim's same-sex partnership. After expressing that appalling sentiment, Robb turned his back on Sally, indicating the conversation was over. Sally grimaced at Robb's crude comments. The company leaders had just been through DEI (diversity, equity, and inclusion) training. Sally had hoped he might have used a more inclusive term and not one that could be perceived as derogatory to a specific culture.

Sally tried one more time to get Robb's attention by saying, "What about Tim? His injuries are serious."

Robb stopped and turned slightly. He then walked to his desk and pushed a button on his desk phone to reach Mary.

"Yes, Robb?"

He directed, "Send Tim some flowers; make sure they are huge arrangements. Yes, I want them to fill the entire room."

Feeling defeated that she hadn't reached Robb at all, Sally left his office.

Case Study 1.2

JEAN-PIERRE MERGENTHALER, known as J.P., led a $1.2 trillion global communications company, Dialogue, Inc., that was the media's darling. Dialogue, Inc. seemed to be untouchable. Regardless of earnings, the stock rose based on Jean-Pierre's grand stories and positive predictions. He knew how to work a press room, and the camera loved him. He was savvy to social media and seemed to say the right things at the right time. The challenge for human resources was that the claims he made weren't always exactly true. Each time J.P. made a statement, fact-checkers would be refuting everything he said. The company's stock price would stumble, and investors worried about the stability of the company.

The CHRO, Melanie Jenkins, would get messages from the Risk Department telling her she needed to put a leash on Jean-Pierre. Melanie was in a delicate situation. She was trying to "manage up." However, she had no direct power or authority over J.P. As a corporate executive, he had control over whether she would retain her job, enjoy an upwardly mobile career path, and receive her annual bonus.

During a high-profile television interview on the weekly live television show *The Sunday Morning Business Review,* J.P. accused a competitor of hacking into Dialogue's computer systems. The interviewer, known for tough questions, pointed out that Dialogue, Inc. seemed to be losing its competitive edge. As Melanie watched the live interview, she noticed that J.P. quickly blinked twice as he said, "That's bullshit; the only way any competitor can beat Dialogue is by cheating. In fact, we have evidence that Global Conference has hacked into our systems."

ORGANIZATIONAL REPERCUSSIONS

Melanie was at home watching the program while wrapped in a fluffy robe, sipping her Sunday morning coffee. The phone rang the minute the words were out of J.P.'s mouth. It was Nidra, the head of corporate counsel. She barked, "Sally, get the transcripts to this show immediately." Sally replied, "Sure, Nidra, I know the drill, but the bigger issue is that J.P. shouldn't be making these kinds of allegations." Nidra replied, "I'm not sure they are untrue. J.P. has a strategic view. There's no way we can all keep up with all that he's doing for Dialogue. We need to trust our leaders." Dumbfounded, Melanie ended the call. She felt like she had nowhere to turn. She witnessed and experienced things that were obviously wrong; however, there was no recourse within her own system. The solution was to "lawyer up" and let the chips fall where they may. The company and many of the employees were enabling the toxic behavior out of fear of losing their jobs.

MELANIE MEETS WITH JEAN-PIERRE

Melanie called J.P. on his cell phone after the event. It was common company knowledge that J.P. didn't read email. He would boast that he deleted anything that came his way. "If it's important, they'll call me!" he'd say with a big grin. Melanie dialed and exclaimed, "J.P., we need to chat!" J.P. replied, "Sure, babe. I am headed to my boat—let's have dinner on my boat." Melanie paused; she didn't want to meet him on his sixty-foot sailboat, *The Destroyer*. She'd been on the boat before for intimate leadership events. J.P. had a passion for fine whiskey, and Melanie didn't drink alcohol. She knew she'd be pressured to try one of his latest finds. Melanie also dreaded being called "babe," although she knew if she didn't tolerate small indiscretions, J.P. would refuse to meet with her, and she'd lose the slight connection she had with him and any hope of influencing him.

Melanie replied to the request with, "Hey, J.P., I'd love to have the opportunity to spend time on your boat. It's just that tonight's not good. I wanted to have a quick chat about *The Sunday Morning Business Review* show. It won't take long." The line went cold. J.P. replied, "What of it?" Melanie pushed on. "Well, Global Conference isn't happy. Social media is exploding, and traditional media channels are starting to investigate." The line went silent again. J.P. finally spoke: "Investigate what?" It was Melanie's turn to go silent now. She wondered if it was possible that he didn't know. She decided to respond exactly to what he had said. "J.P., they want to investigate the claim you made on *The Sunday Morning Business Review* that Global Conference had hacked into Dialogue's systems." J.P. bellowed, "I never said that." Melanie retorted, "Well, it's in the transcript." J.P. volleyed back, "It's a lie.

"Melanie, you just don't have what it takes to work at a progressive company like Dialogue. We need leaders. I've been trying to get rid of you for ages." Melanie was stunned. She needed this job. She did her best to compose herself and replied, "The stock is down a hundred points today, and we've received a call that the SEC (Securities and Exchange Commission) wants to investigate Dialogue's practices. The new chief operations officer we extended an offer to has rescinded his acceptance of the employment offer we made."

J.P. rolled his eyes. "Like I said, you have no idea what you are doing. Your whining proves it. Have Nidra call me."

Case Study 1.3

GARY BASKIN had been CHRO since the inception of the ten-year-old billion-dollar technology company AI Robotics. The freewheeling, casual behaviors that had created the company's initial success were now becoming liabilities. The founding partners, Chad Landan and Taylor Miranda, were so close they could read each other's minds. They made decisions from their guts, took significant risks, and were able to identify opportunities most people weren't even thinking about yet. The cash flooded in, and, as a result, AI Robotics' infrastructure was weak. Processes were loose, and many talented employees couldn't handle the "fly by the seat of your pants and see if it works" work environment.

Taylor and Chad met Lily Franklin at an online hackathon. They loved Lily's ability to take risks, and she was aligned with their intuitive communication style. They seemed to get each other. Taylor and Chad made Lily the face of AI Robotics. She was the key media contact. They created a Lily Franklin Excellence Award, which would be granted to employees who demonstrated outstanding achievements. Lily beamed at each level of recognition. She loved being in the spotlight and couldn't get enough.

The employees called Lily "Supergirl," after the superhero comic book published by DC Comics. Lily held several technology patents, could match anyone drink for drink during happy hours, and operated on a few hours' sleep. It wasn't unusual for her team to receive an email from her at 2:00 a.m. or a random phone call during the weekend. Lily didn't have a home base. She thought of herself as a global citizen and arranged long-term rentals around the world. Her thought process was that, through technology, she was always connected, so it didn't matter where she lived. While there was some truth to that, the employees never knew Lily's whereabouts. Managing all the time zones was chaotic. They weren't sure if they could include her in in-person meetings. Employees never knew what to expect.

Lily participated in extreme-sports events during her time off, including windsurfing, mountain climbing, and ultra-marathons. Once she suggested her direct reports go skydiving with her as a team builder. A couple went, but others flatly refused. One employee asked, "Why should I jump out of a perfectly good airplane?"

Gary agreed Lily was extreme, but she was a rock star. If he could bottle her super-intelligence and share it with the others, life at the company would be great. To make the situation worse for Gary, Lily was a very likable woman. The trouble was that no one could work with her. Talented people could not keep up; others were smart, but Lily was gifted.

Employees were taking leaves of absences to avoid being around Lily. Office gossip was rampant, hurting productivity. Insurance costs were surprisingly high for such a young workforce. There were claims for anxiety-related illnesses. Once employees completed a project and stacked their resumes, they quickly left AI Robotics for new and better positions.

Lily was adamant that she wanted to surround herself with winners. She couldn't tolerate those who couldn't keep up. She always had a quick reason why others were not capable. She loved her rock-star status and enjoyed touting her superiority over others.

According to the current human-resources policy, the only way to allow Lily to retain the managing-partner position at the firm was to have her manage at least six subordinates. The company's private investors and the board could not justify paying Lily a significant salary without what they considered to be a leadership contribution. Chad and Taylor didn't have an opinion either way. They had let go of the reins of control of the company long ago. At this point, the executive leadership team attempted to watch them as best they could while keeping an eye on damage control. The greatest risk at this point was Lily.

ORGANIZATIONAL REPERCUSSIONS

AI Robotics had to pay significant signing bonuses to recruit new employees. They were paying much more than their competitor, however, it was necessary to provide a bonus because of the erratic work environment. AI Robotics was creating evolving technology, and they needed the talent, so they justified the cost. Lily, Chad, and Taylor thought the bonuses were a great recruiting tool and were happy with the employees enticed by the attractive financial incentives.

None of the leaders, however, realized that those funds could be invested in creating efficient operations, enabling long-term growth and a sustainable competitive advantage. The company culture was loose and freewheeling and seemed to be an extension of wild university days. The company parties were legendary, with stories of intimate encounters and rumors of illegal substances, which were nightmares for HR. Nothing, at this point, could be proven. Gary slept with one eye open, waiting for something to blow up.

Employees were not performing optimally in the frenzied environment. They felt frazzled under Lily's leadership, never knowing what was expected. Since the company had grown so fast, rewards were granted randomly. There were spot bonuses and stories of great achievements. The company ran on folklore. Unfortunately, any employee who did a great job had no idea how to repeat their success.

Employees passed around names of recruiters who were hungry for AI Robotics' proprietary technology. The intellectual property that propelled the organization was at risk. Unfortunately, Chad, Taylor, and Lily didn't realize that their competitive advantage was slipping right out the door with the wisdom of their short-term employees. The employees who stayed stuck with AI Robotics for the good salaries. The company culture was full of directionless activity. While the company was randomly successful, the costs of turnover, healthcare, and recruiting fees—and AI Robotics' wild reputation—were serious operational risks.

GARY TRIES TO COACH LILY

Gary was struggling with what to do. His challenge was that there was no perceived problem. It was impossible to solve a problem that hadn't been defined. However, Gary took his role seriously and understood AI Robotics' great potential. He wanted to be part of the company's success. Developing robots powered by artificial intelligence is exciting. Gary didn't want to sit on the sidelines knowing he hadn't given solving these behavioral problems his best shot.

He tracked Lily down on her way to Antarctica. She was preparing to do extreme-weather scuba diving. She assured Gary she could take a video meeting while she traveled. When Gary called, and Lily picked up, he saw her long hair flowing as she jostled with the weight of her backpack. She appeared to be walking outside, but Gary wasn't sure where she was. Gary asked, "Lily? Are you sure this is a good time?"

"Yes! Yes! What's up?"

Gary paused, trying to maintain control, not sure if it was possible to have a conversation in this environment. "Well, Lily, we're in a state of extreme growth at AI Robotics."

She interrupted, "Right, right. I get that."

He went on, "The signing bonuses are incomparable in the marketplace."

"Great! We are attracting the best talent. Gary, I appreciate you so much!" Lily said while juggling her backpack. Finally, Gary watched her image bounce all over the telephone screen as she trekked through a rugged path. Gary turned the video off so he could focus on the conversation and avoid the distracting image.

"Sure, Lily, it *is* great—however, I think we can reduce that expense." Lily was entirely unaware of how her behavior was affecting employees and impacting the company's bottom line.

"I'm not tracking; we have plenty of money. We are in uncharted territory. This is not time to be meek or conservative." Gary winced a little, wondering if the words "meek" and "conservative" were jabs at him, someone who could not and would never dive in Antarctica. "Well, Lily, there are ways to be wise with resources, and I thought you might want to brainstorm about it one day."

"You got it!" she replied. "I'll ping you when I get back!"

Gary was frustrated as he ended the call. He didn't know when Lily would be back. When she returned, he wasn't sure he'd be able to pin her down for a time to have a meaningful conversation about resources.

———

The stories described here are real. While the names were changed and the situations were enhanced, they are, unfortunately, common, real occurrences from my case files. In these case studies, the senior leaders, Robb, J.P., and Lily, demonstrated some of the characteristics of narcissistic behavior, which include:

- an exaggerated sense of self-importance

- a lack of integrity

- a tendency to lie in order to manipulate facts in their favor

- a sense of entitlement requiring constant, excessive admiration

- expecting to be recognized as superior even without achievements that warrant it

- exaggerating achievements and talents

- believing they are superior and can associate only with equally special people

- monopolizing conversations and belittling or looking down on people they perceive as inferior

- expecting special favors and unquestioning compliance with their expectations

- bullying behavior

- using human resource policies designed to protect employee rights as weapon to manipulate or bully direct reports to maintain power in their command and control leadership style

- taking advantage of others to get what they want

- an inability or unwillingness to recognize the needs and feelings of others

- being envious of others and believing others envy them

- behaving in an arrogant or haughty manner; coming across as conceited, boastful, and pretentious

- insisting on having the best of everything—for instance, the best car or office

Unfortunately, I've witnessed many other stories like this during my career, which spans three decades working with companies of all sizes. As listed above, the narcissistic leader will have an exaggerated sense of self-importance. They will quickly take credit for achievements and consistently run loose with details. Robb Lockett has these characteristics. He wants to make sure everyone knows he is always the BOSS—not really a leader, but that he has command and control of the people and things around him. Robb also demands to be recognized even when his achievements don't warrant recognition.

While Lily is pleasant, her antics garner constant admiration. She's been written up in magazine articles, and conversations generally lead to whatever exotic activity she is currently engaged in. There's a need for continuous admiration and attention. Lily is the type of person who wants attention and will accept it from anyone . . . even when she knows she does not deserve it. This is also a characteristic of narcissistic personality disorder. While Lily is fun to be around, she does have a sense of entitlement. She needs to be the star and is not willing to share the limelight with others. Lily's extreme behavior ensures she is always in the spotlight.

J.P. is so good at exaggerating his talents, he's frequently featured in the media, and the spotlight easily shines on him. That's great for shareholders but not so great for those who rely on him and interact with him daily. This toxic behavior, which is often dismissed as "JP being JP," is a very serious example of people around him being enablers of toxic-leader behaviors, which leads to a systemic toxic culture.

You may recognize people exhibiting other characteristics of narcissism, for instance, individuals who need to monopolize conversations and belittle others they perceive as inferior. The only way a narcissist can feel as if they are a ten on a ten-point scale is if everyone around them feels like a five. A narcissistic leader thinks that just about everyone is inferior to them, so this behavior should be pretty easy to spot. Narcissistic leaders will also expect special favors from others. They expect and demand to be treated as if they are uniquely distinguished leaders. The narcissistic leader usually has a tight inner circle. They surround themselves with people who will unquestioningly comply with their expectations. These supporters who enable the toxic leader's behavior often either hope to ride the coattails of the toxic leader to the top for their own careers or are extremely insecure and afraid to challenge or show disapproval. Narcissistic toxic leaders take advantage of others to get what they want. Since they surround themselves with people who will tolerate this behavior, they are forgiven, or their behavior is justified, allowing them to move forward. They are famous for promising bonuses or promotions to those loyal to them; the bonuses and promotions rarely materialize. Still, the narcissistic toxic leader believes they are justified and continues their path. Narcissists have a clear lack of empathy. They lack awareness and are either unable or unwilling to recognize the feelings and needs of others. In the narcissistic toxic leader's world, others are not important. The leader with a narcissistic personality disorder has an excessively positive self-regard and rejects suggestions that challenge this viewpoint. In psychology, they are seen as being ego-syntonic because they are unaware of, and unfazed by, how others view their behavior. This corresponds to the general concept known as "having poor insight." Narcissistic leaders often accuse others of being jealous of them. They are generally arrogant and can come across as conceited, boastful, and pretentious. Material things are essential to narcissists. You'll find them driving the latest car, living in an exclusive area, and ordering the best bottle of champagne at lunch. The narcissist will demand a prestigious office or a vacation in a place where high-profile celebrities vacation. During an interview, they may ask questions about the office, support, and amenities they will receive.

Narcissistic leaders present a challenge to chief human resources officers because of their position and status. They are also challenging because they will have trouble handling any communication they perceive as criticism. The narcissistic leader will become impatient or angry when they don't receive special treatment. They are known to terminate employees on the spot; others unwilling to tolerate the tirades walk out. Narcissistic leaders will hold a grudge. They will let you and anyone else know if they've been offended. When narcissistic toxic leaders feel attacked, they will react with rage or contempt, belittling the person they are dealing with in order to feel superior. Narcissistic leaders will work to restore their feelings of superiority to defend themselves against someone they perceive is receiving more attention than them. They continually draw attention to themselves as a means of keeping employees off balance. When feeling challenged, the narcissistic leader will have difficulty regulating their emotions and behavior. The narcissistic leader will demand to know about any change that might be coming their way. They will surround themselves with trusted confidants to ensure they will never be surprised by the news. When the narcissistic leader is caught off guard, they will have difficulty dealing with the stress and adapting to the change. At times, the narcissistic leader will fall into a depression and have periods of unpredictable moodiness when they suspect they are falling far from perfection. One interesting quality about narcissistic leaders is that their larger-than-life behaviors cover secret feelings of shame, vulnerability, and humiliation.

THE ORIGINS OF THE TERM "NARCISSIST"

The disorder is named after the Greek god Narcissus, the hunter.

According to myth, the Oread nymph Echo spotted Narcissus while he was hunting. Echo immediately fell in love with the handsome Narcissus. When Echo was near Narcissus, she attempted to hug him. Narcissus pushed Echo away, not interested in her advances at all. Echo, filled with despair, roamed the woods, mourning the loss of Narcissus's love for the remainder of her life, ultimately wilting away until all that was left of her was a faint echo sound.

When Nemesis, the goddess of retribution and revenge, learned how Narcissus had treated Echo, she set out to punish him for his cruelty. Narcissus's punishment would be that each time he saw his reflection in a pool of water, he would fall in love with it. Narcissus, unaware that the person he was in love with was merely his own reflection, ultimately killed himself, suffering from unrequited love.

The story of Narcissus in Greek myth helps us to easily recognize the symptoms of narcissistic personality disorder. According to the *Diagnostic and Statistical Manual of Mental Disorders (DSM)*, people with narcissistic personality disorder (NPD) are characterized by certain personality traits, including persistent grandiosity, excessive need for admiration, and a lack of empathy for other people.

HOW TO INTERACT WITH A NARCISSISTIC LEADER

Although, as stated previously, HR executives are sometimes reduced to putting out corporate fires, managing risk, and recruiting and terminating employees, they have the power to elevate their role. Savvy HR executives and business partners will recognize that their role is more critical than ever.

Employees want flexibility, transparency, and the ability to be themselves at work. They demand that their employers also recognize that they have personal lives. Additionally, employees want to be respected by leadership and treated as partners. The old "command and control" style of leadership is obsolete.

Stephen M.R. Covey shared in his book *Trust and Inspire* that the command and control style of leadership has become increasingly more ineffective in our dynamic, multi-generational, interconnected world. His research of thousands of leaders from some top companies in the world states the vast majority of people still say the primarily leadership style is command and control. I believe this style comes in play because many leaders have only seen this style modeled in the workplace and it has been rewarded in our pay for performance culture. While you don't have to have a personality disorder to practice the command and control leadership style, it is clear to me that when a personality disorder is in play the impact on the team and organization is more pronounced.

The economy is global. Employees network everywhere, making guarding corporate trade secrets increasingly impossible. The HR executive has the opportunity to review these challenges and embrace them as opportunities. This is a new territory, and HR, for the first time since the Industrial Age began, has the opportunity to lead the way.

These case studies are based on real situations. I'll share some strategies detailing how I have worked within these situations. I have decades of experience receiving calls from organizational consultants and HR professionals like Sally, Greg, and Melanie. Enhancing an organizational structure in a time of significant change is not a simple task. It will take a team of aligned professionals to influence positive change. HR professionals are not therapists. However, understanding personality disorders enables them to spot behaviors that create a toxic narcissistic environment.

I've outlined some resources and tools I use to *work with* the narcissistic leader versus attempting to *change the leader*. Ideally, if these tactics are employed properly, the leader may recognize their behaviors and realize that, to continue to rise to higher levels of success, they'll have to adapt and implement new behaviors.

HR must proactively drive to implement well-thought-out, meticulously drafted policies. If HR says there is an open-door, confidential policy, they must really have one. They may have the right tools—but they won't have teeth unless they are enforced.

DON'T TOLERATE INAPPROPRIATE LANGUAGE

Many people suffer from inappropriate statements or actions. During the last twenty years, many of us have witnessed a devolution of appropriate, acceptable behavior in the workplace. What was "okay" twenty years ago is not tolerable today. We have as many as five generations in the workforce. Yes, many older workers have reached very senior levels, and many of these are white males. Since they've been in positions of power, common practices may have evaded them. Executive coaches help leaders adapt to worldwide cultures. HR leaders can help senior leaders adapt to appropriate behavior to advance a positive corporate culture.

Robb Lockett should not make derogatory statements about the LGBTQIA community or women. J.P.'s perspective might be that it's flattering and warm to address Melanie as "babe." If she doesn't find a way to let him know it's not okay, in a way he won't feel attacked by, this behavior will continue.

Learning new skills to influence positive behavior in narcissistic leaders is necessary as the world advances in unpredictable ways at record speed. Here's a tip that works for tough conversations: all these conversations work best one-on-one and in person. Email can be dismissed or misinterpreted. Narcissistic leaders must be retrained through standard leadership-development programs; depending on the severity of the toxicity, weekly coaching from either internal or external professionals will help create higher levels of awareness.

IDENTIFY NARCISSISTIC BEHAVIORS

The leader will show signs of narcissism early on. A clear indication is the inability to accept criticism and feedback, which means they lack personal and professional awareness. If an organizational consultant or HR professional attempts to address the issues, they are often viciously verbally attacked. Narcissists play dirty. It's difficult for the most seasoned organizational consultant or HR professional to deal with. This is why I recommend that only well-trained practitioners with a combination of organizational and clinical skills be used to remediate this type of toxic leader or coach you as an HR professional on how to engage.

If the leader is argumentative or dismissive, this might be a sign that they have a narcissistic personality disorder. If they are grandiose and constantly seek attention, they could have a narcissistic personality disorder. Sometimes people have more than one personality disorder. Narcissists often have borderline personality disorder, too. They will vacillate between extremes and see the world as black-and-white or pass/fail. Identifying and working with borderline personality disorder will be covered more thoroughly in the next section.

Lily seems to have elements of borderline personality and demonstrates manic behavior with her unpredictability and constant stream of energy. Employees will constantly be on their heels, attempting to predict what Lily might want or do next. No employee will be able to perform consistently in this environment. Lily's direct reports feel as if they are firefighters. There's always a crisis that needs to be addressed; they just don't know what it will be, how big, or how long it will last.

BE PROACTIVE, NOT REACTIVE

Don't wait for the inventible tragedy to happen or for the bad press. The leaders of the organization have put you in your spot for a reason. Tip others off to the fact that there might be a problem. Practice and learn diplomacy skills. It's critical to be accepted as a trusted advisor. No one will trust an HR executive they perceive will one day turn against them. Here's a sample conversation to try in Lily's scenario.

"Chad and Taylor, Lily is such an asset to our organization." *They will likely agree.* "The problem is, not many of our employees can keep up with Supergirl." *Suggest an alternative solution.* "AI Robotics' rule of having a leader have direct reports doesn't seem to be relevant." *They may become defensive or confused. Gary can now plant seeds for new ideas.* "We are an artificial-intelligence company that uses robotics; we are leading the way in the new frontier of technology. Our HR solutions need to match our technological progress." *Gary might capture their attention with this positioning.* "I have a plan." *Most leaders will be receptive to a person with a plan.* "What if we relieve Lily of her direct reports while I design some infrastructure? We can put her on a special assignment, where we play to her strengths. We need her. It doesn't have to be forever. I'd like to repurpose some of the budget we are losing and redirect it to retention." *Gary shares recent competitive data showing that AI Robotics is losing its edge.* "Our intellectual property is slipping out the door."

It might work, and it might not. But, by having this proactive conversation with the company's founders, Gary is positioning himself as a strategic leader and elevating himself as someone who picks up the pieces and manages the chaos.

Inform other leaders in the company of the warning signs and what could happen as a result of ignoring damaging behavior. You are the expert in human resources—the person best positioned to suggest and design solutions. Create a list of allies throughout all levels of the organization who will help you influence change.

DON'T BE SEDUCED BY PROMISES

We perceive that senior leaders hold the keys to our careers, financial advancement, and professional advancement. While that may be true, what job is worth having an accident like Tim's on their conscience? In addition, who wants to miss the opportunity to do the job they longed to do? People rarely go to college, study a field, and then determine that all they can do is go along to get along.

Pay attention to whether other people are accepting unacceptable behavior. Do not enable the narcissistic leader's behavior. Provide coaching to leaders and employees who have to deal with challenging behavior. Support each other. Have open communications through informal meetings and communication channels. Don't wait for things to blow up on social media.

RAGE AND RETALIATION

The narcissistic leader will not receive any conversations about changing their behavior well. Be prepared for intimidation tactics or blatant insults. Be confident in your career and your choices. There are no secure jobs, however, HR executives are in control of their careers. Remember, with every action you take, you are building your personal brand. If the company you are working for does not endorse your solutions, be prepared with your own exit strategy.

Practice what you want to say to the narcissistic leader. Role-play it with a trusted colleague. Use difficult-conversation methods to stay focused. You may still be nervous; however, the practice will put you in a position to remain in command, ultimately being more effective. Have a third party present in the room. Document meetings. It's especially easy to do with video calls these days. Be prepared with strategies to deflect the situation if the narcissistic leader starts to belittle you. The narcissistic leader might use a hostile tone or intimidating body language. Their reactions will be predictors of future reactions. You can expect this behavior the next time something doesn't go their way. Take time to reflect on the behaviors, and plan your actions.

DON'T QUESTION YOURSELF

A senior leader's job is to ensure an organization is agile and can pivot when required. Their job is to design a Ferrari, not plug along in a mini-van. Senior leaders with personality disorders poison the organization and prevent them from flourishing and growing.

Organizations today have to respond quickly to market demands. There are no shortcuts. Toxic behavior is an ugly underbelly that creates a cancerous web of dysfunction. The companies that were the most successful through the pandemic were agile, nimble, and capable of developing new solutions to market conditions. Employees in companies that successfully transformed were innovative and free to make smart decisions. They lived the mission statement; it wasn't just a plaque on the wall. They could be just as effective in a virtual environment as they were pre-pandemic, or even more so. Many organizations did a great job redefining their operations and sales culture when they could no longer meet in person or conduct face-to-face sales calls.

SUCCESSFULLY INFLUENCE THE NARCISSISTIC LEADER

As stated earlier, do not attempt to change the behavior or fix the leader. Instead, *work with* the leader's personality to create increased self-awareness, so they understand how they show up and the impact that it will have on their legacy as a good leader. Most narcissists can't stand thinking that they are not the best at what they do, including leading their organization.

Understand the business you are in. Human resources can no longer just focus on the human component. You will gain the senior leader's respect by understanding the business you are in. Avoid a linear career path, and branch out by attending conferences and reading books. Learn about your competitors. Understand the business from a wider perspective, including how effective talent management will help the company advance.

ENGAGE THE LEADER

While Melanie didn't want to drink alcohol and detested being called "babe," she didn't scold J.P. or argue with him. She used some avoidance tactics but also did her best to influence him by sticking to the facts and the goal of the conversation. Melanie stood firm on her principles and did not allow herself to be pulled into his behavior. While the narcissistic leader will often struggle to accept reality, it may be her only defense when he tries to pass blame on to her when negative consequence come his way. Don't be afraid to engage in straight talk during meetings when the opportunity presents itself. Don't allow yourself to be bullied; call out disrespectful behaviors in real time. However, this must be done strategically to have the desired impact and avoid giving the toxic leader a stage on which to perform. Hopefully, in the future, this will no longer be necessary. As HR leaders take courageous stands and strive to create organizations that operate effectively, the workforce will become more productive over time.

We would never put up with what our parents tolerated in the workforce. The younger people in our lives will likely shake their heads in wonder at the way generations before them interacted. We know for sure the world grows and changes. We have more access to resources and information than ever. We can do our best to influence positivity by building a foundation for a stronger future.

PRACTICE CONVERSATIONS AND ROLE-PLAY INTERACTIONS

Stay strong, and take care of yourself, including your own mental health. Narcissistic leaders are masters at understanding and exploiting weakness. Was Gary onto something when he thought Lily was mocking him by suggesting he was "meek" and "conservative"? Probably. Since Gary knows that she will do this, he can be prepared the next time he talks to her. He might make a gentle joke or ignore the comment altogether. By focusing on the growth opportunity for AI Robotics, Gary has the opportunity to help Lily see herself leading that success. The world is not fair, but it's still good. He may have to tolerate a few jabs to get Lily to focus on the company's growth and maximize her talents.

RECOGNIZE THE POSITIVITY

Sally has her work cut out for her with Robb. He is a seemingly unstoppable force who has kicked many people stronger and smarter than Sally to the curb, while trudging forward with no awareness of his damaging behavior. Unfortunately, Robb is the manifestation of the systems that accepted and perhaps endorsed his behavior. Robb may have been rewarded in his family, the schools he attended, the sports teams he played for, and the companies he's worked with. World Innovation Solutions probably went to great lengths and authorized a significant financial investment to recruit him. Sally will have to do her best to engage Robb, understand the business she's in, and practice potential conversations.

Any one of these leaders may bring in a consultant to help with the situation. As Robb Lockett stated, sending out an RFP is a pretty common solution. The organizational-development consultant will have a greater chance of success when they partner with an informed HR leader who has explored every possibility to work with the toxic senior leader. A cohesive team of HR professionals has a greater chance to influence positive change.

———————

Chances are that the toxic senior leader wants to do a great job. They want to be successful; the behaviors they've developed *have* created success for them. Some narcissistic leaders will change when a company explodes or when they find themselves in the midst of a scandal. However, it doesn't have to get that drastic. It is possible to influence these powerful people to be more beneficial for all and create a stronger organization.

Personality disorders are not exclusive of one another. For example, a leader may have elements of narcissistic personality disorder, borderline personality disorder, and passive-aggressive disorder. Lily demonstrated aspects of borderline personality. Interacting with leaders who have borderline personality disorder is explored in an upcoming section.

The Passive-Aggressive Leader

IT MIGHT SEEM HARD TO BELIEVE, but there is a benefit to working with a narcissistic leader—they are easy to spot. Narcissistic leaders' extreme behavior—where they constantly draw attention to themselves, portray themselves as a lone star, and squash others for their own benefit—is almost caricatural. It's well-documented that the forty-fifth president of the United States, Donald J. Trump, displayed extremely narcissistic behaviors. In public appearances, he called people names, mocked them, and would walk off the stage when things were not going his way. He famously used the social-media platform Twitter (now know as X) to fire people. Executives had no idea that they'd been unceremoniously released from their position unless they happened to be on social media, saw it on the news, or learned the shocking news from someone else. The president appeared to delight in humiliating anyone who disagreed with him or made him seem less powerful in any way. Regardless of your political beliefs or opinions of the president's performance, his narcissistic behaviors are now part of recorded history.

Accomplished and notable professionals who report to toxic leaders endure these behaviors because they are crippled by fear. They worry they could lose their jobs, dread being humiliated in public, and hesitate to argue openly with an influential leader. In addition, they may be driven by a sense of duty. The toxic leader's direct reports and others who have tolerated the abusive behavior have an opportunity to influence positive change if they stay inside the system. If they are dismissed, the tyrannical toxic leader will have even more power because newer employees may be less adept at dealing with challenging behavior.

Healthy, grounded senior leaders would never behave in this way. The conduct the president displayed is destructive. Furthermore, these actions are unacceptable for the leader of the free world, who has the power to influence societal advancement.

The dilemma with personality disorders is that the senior leaders afflicted with maladaptive actions produce results. Another notable narcissist was Steve Jobs. Known for his charismatic and persuasive ability to communicate, he also had a dark side, which is described in the biography *Steve Jobs*, written by Walter Isaacson and published by Thorndike Press in 2011. The comprehensive volume is based on forty exclusive and unprecedented interviews with Steve Jobs himself.

Jobs was so enamored with his brilliance that he was ultimately fired from Apple, the very company he created. Isaacson's book on Jobs provides accounts from people who worked with him, relaying that Jobs lacked empathy for people and consistently bullied and exploited those around him. The testimony conveys that he was also arrogant, controlling, and manipulative. While it's likely that these stories are true, there's no denying his brilliance. Cell phones that could take photographs and play music were unimaginable before Steve Jobs had the creativity to explore what adding these features might accomplish in the development of the iPhone.

After being dismissed from Apple, Jobs went on to create another hardware and software enterprise known as NeXT, Inc. The company initially floundered. However, ironically, Apple eventually acquired NeXT, Inc. in 1996 for $429 million.

In 1986, Jobs purchased the computer-graphics division from Lucasfilm Ltd. from entrepreneur, filmmaker, producer, and screenwriter George Lucas for $5 million. At the time, the company, which would be renamed Pixar, had only forty employees. Steve Jobs grew the company and ultimately revolutionized animation. As of 2022, Pixar was valued at $8 billion and employed more than 1,200 people.

Bottom-line results rule in our capitalist society. However, there are ways to achieve greatness without crushing those around you. Unfortunately, our culture is so accustomed to toxic activities, at times we justify the approach and minimize the impact of negative behaviors, excusing those who are producing results. I call these supporters *toxic enablers*.

Balanced senior leaders inspire the potential of their teams and all of those they interact with by using four elements of leadership: trust, autonomy, communication, and accountability. Senior leaders who are aware of their shortcomings recognize that there is limitless possibility for achievement when each employee's strengths are fully implemented. Unhealthy senior leaders work in isolation or secrecy. They may have a very tight circle of people they trust, to whom they will divulge select information.

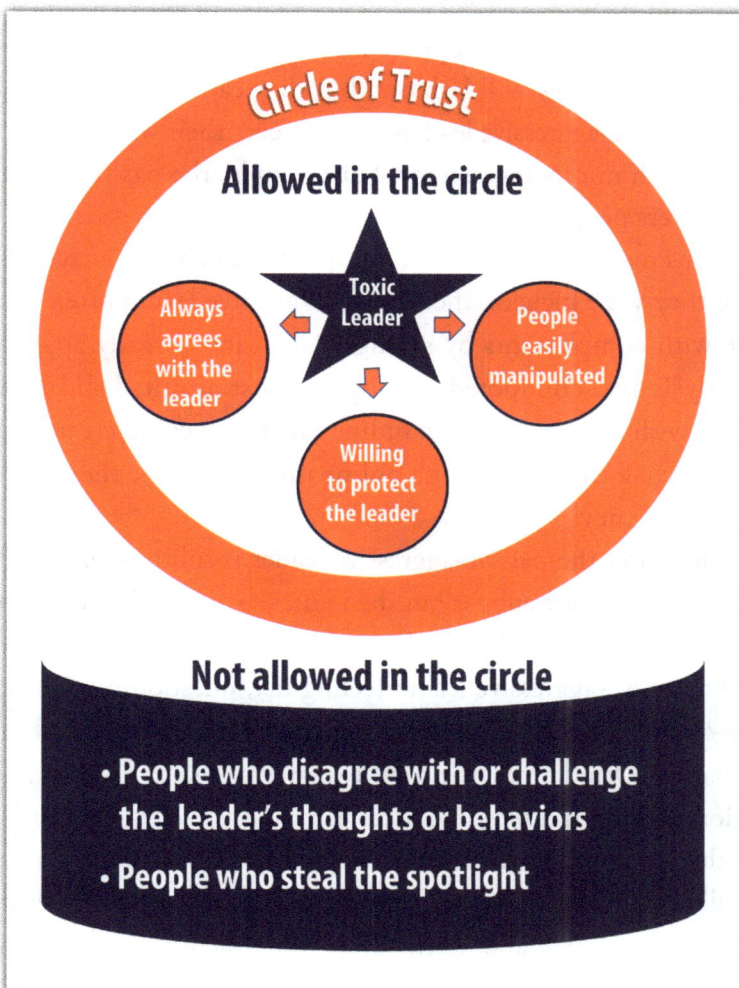

Circle of Trust

Allowed in the circle

Toxic Leader

Always agrees with the leader

People easily manipulated

Willing to protect the leader

Not allowed in the circle

- People who disagree with or challenge the leader's thoughts or behaviors
- People who steal the spotlight

Toxic senior leaders are masters of maneuvering through situations and deceit. The great poet and civil-rights activist Maya Angelou famously stated, "People will forget what you said, but they will never forget how you made them feel." Toxic senior leaders know this and use their ability to make people feel good to their advantage. They calculate ways to make those around them feel confident that they have their best interests at heart. The toxic senior leader will then turn on those who trust them, even the people in their inner circle, leaving them to wonder what happened.

Narcissistic leaders are openly mean and nasty. Those who work with them know they will lash out, but they cannot predict when. In contrast, passive-aggressive leaders are indirect. Their words and actions are filled with micro-aggressions. For example, the passive-aggressive leader butters people up and then kicks them without warning. Their aggressions may be so subtle, the victim of the behavior may not even be sure they were kicked! The passive-aggressive leader often showers people with compliments by saying, "Great job. I really appreciated the analysis you conducted. Though I must admit, I didn't think someone with a degree from an online university could create impressive results like these. Although online universities are the way of the future, aren't they?"

In this case, the passive-aggressive leader is subtly suggesting that online universities are subpar but then quickly adds, "it's the way of the future." The actions are barely detectable, leaving people who interact with the passive-aggressive leader feeling flat, questioning themselves, and re-evaluating their behaviors. Sometimes there's a little jab in the conversation. Other times, the passive-aggressive leader displays positive behavior, making it difficult to ascertain what is really going on.

If the passive-aggressive leader is confronted about the statement, they will be prepared with a perfectly plausible explanation. For example, suppose the comment about attending an online university is brought to the attention of someone in the human-resources department. In that case, the passive-aggressive leader will likely respond by acting confused. They will explain how they encourage all employees to advance their education. They'll note that the company provides tuition reimbursement and that they have approved tens of thousands of dollars for employees to improve themselves. They'll discuss how they recently took an online course provided by Harvard and that it was excellent. Finally, they might act offended, causing the human-resources representative to apologize to *them*. After a situation like this occurs, the employee who was mocked will be less likely to report a transgression in the future. They will avoid risk by becoming an underperforming employee. Lack of contribution will become a method of survival in a broken organization. The constant uncertainty will perpetuate organizational customs and behaviors, enabling passive-aggressive behaviors to become an acceptable norm. More employees will observe what works and begin to mirror the maladaptive behavior.

There's an old comedy sketch from the 1930s made famous by the vaudevillian comedians Abbott & Costello. It's known as "Who's on First?" The comedians parody a baseball game. The first-base player's name is Who, the second-base player's name is What, and the third-base player's name is I Don't Know. Abbott asks, "Who's on First?" Costello replies, "I don't know." Exasperated, Abbott responds, "I Don't Know is on Third!" The comedians go round and round. It's funny to watch but difficult to live through.

The passive-aggressive leader will act in similar ways demonstrated by the old classic comedy sketch. They'll tell people one thing and do another. They may blatantly lie or deny certain actions, even when there's proof of their maladaptive behavior. They will be so persuasive, passionate, and convincing that their employees and colleagues may start to believe the lie they are telling in the moment. The employees and colleagues will grow frustrated, question their own ability to understand a situation, and operate in a state of confusion, unsure what they need to do to be successful.

IDENTIFYING THE DARK SIDE OF PERSONALITY

Toxic leaders have developed a mastery of presenting themselves in a positive light. As a result, they constantly tout a string of successes. They are engaging, accomplished, admired, and aggressively sought after for coveted roles. The Hogan Assessment is a resource that can be used to uncover how the leader will perform under stressful situations, where they feel they are being attacked or out of control.

The Hogan Assessment was established by the husband-and-wife team of Drs. Joyce and Robert Hogan in 1987. The assessment has been used in fifty-six countries and has been translated into forty-seven languages. More than half of the Fortune 500 companies have used the assessment. I find the assessment's information enlightening in hiring leaders, managing them, providing course correction when situations go awry, and teaching their teams to perform under seemingly unpredictable circumstances.

The assessment correlates passive-aggressive behavior with the label *Leisurely*. From a therapeutic perspective, the underlying circumstances of the passive-aggressive leader may have, at one time, been immersed in a culture of positive attention and warmth. Many times, the individual experienced an extreme, abrupt change that destroyed their stable world. The crisis could have occurred in childhood or adulthood. In childhood, it's possible that a loving home was disrupted by divorce, the death of a parent, or the death of a beloved grandparent, which created a sense of upheaval in the passive-aggressive leader's life. In adulthood, transitioning from the sure path of academia to the uncertain environment of a corporate setting could be unsettling for someone with passive-aggressive tendencies. The clues to look for when identifying a passive-aggressive leader are monitoring their behavior when they are in a favorable, predictable situation and then when they transition to an unstable, unpredictable situation.

When the passive-aggressive leader is in an environment they feel comfortable in, they will be quite pleasant to be around. In a stable situation, they will be helpful, positive, cooperative, and responsive to feedback and coaching. They are often engaging, open to feedback, steady, and forgiving. They are often comfortable expressing emotions. Passive-aggressive leaders are efficient, reliable, and willing to help others in situations where they feel they are in control. They believe their hard work will speak for itself.

Furthermore, if the passive-aggressive leader feels they are in control of a situation, they will be flexible when demands change and a new performance is required. The passive-aggressive leader typically has many friends and advocates, as they are cheerful and optimistic. They will be helpful to others when their colleagues are experiencing personal issues or are overloaded with tasks and crushing deadlines. On their best day, the passive-aggressive leader will seem like the ideal leader.

Since their toxic behaviors are so difficult to identify, those with passive-aggressive personality disorder are common throughout organizations. They are particularly loved when they are at the C-level of organizations and difficult to coach. Many times, organizations lack organizational-development professionals and coaches who have the skill set to influence high-level leaders. In addition, the passive-aggressive leader often has a strong constituency of passionate supporters. When toxic behavior is identified, the supporters will rally to the defense of the passive-aggressive toxic leader, which further enables the toxic behavior and helps fortify the toxic culture. The advocates are so enthralled with the passive-aggressive leader's demonstration of kindness and compassion that they overlook toxic actions. In addition, culturally, we are so uncomfortable with confrontation and accountability that we endure toxic leaders, allowing broken organizations to evolve around them.

The dark side of the passive-aggressive toxic leader's behavior includes valuing their independence so much that they covertly resist requests from others. No one will know what is going on, as plans and decisions are made in a shroud of secrecy. Chances are, the passive-aggressive leader does not know what is going on themselves. They are attempting to figure out solutions, and once they do, they may or may not share their ideas with others. Conversely, they will complain, "I have to do everything myself!" Passive-aggressive toxic leaders appear to be warm and friendly, however, they do not trust other people's abilities. They perceive that they are the only ones who can come in and save the day for the company in any situation.

Employees and peers will struggle as the passive-aggressive leader does not clearly communicate expectations. Their vague, positive expressions will leave the employees feeling like they are on the right track. However, the bewildered subordinate will struggle with constantly being wrong and continually missing the mark. The passive-aggressive leader may become easily annoyed with interruptions, leaving the employees reluctant to ask questions or challenge the status quo. They may say they have an open-door policy but are impossible to reach. Ultimately, the employees will start to refrain from submitting ideas or suggestions, knowing it's best to wait to see if there is consistent information they can count on from the passive-aggressive leader. The employees mimic the passive-aggressive behaviors demonstrated by the leader. They will stop suggesting ideas or making contributions, causing organizational progress to stall.

The following case study is based on real situations I've witnessed in my experience as a clinician and an organizational-development consultant working with toxic senior leaders. I've provided insights in italics to help clearly identify the passive-aggressive behaviors in the situation.

IT STARTS AT THE TOP

Silver Creek Community Trust (SCCT) is a legacy nonprofit started a hundred years ago in Summit City, Missouri, a town with a population of approximately seventy-eight thousand. The area has big-city resources with a small-town feel. Everyone seems to know everyone else in one way or another. SCCT provides resources and services to the community, including child-care resources, advanced-education scholarships, travel opportunities, family support, and elder-care services. SCCT is the pride of the community. When the time came to replace the longtime CEO, the board decided it would be necessary to conduct a nationwide search to bring the best talent to their intimate town.

The board members thought of their work with SCCT as a call. The members were honored to serve their community and were actively involved. After several months of interviews and screenings, they unanimously decided to hire Claire Davis. They were sure Claire was perfect for the role.

Claire had just published a book entitled *To Live Is to Serve*. Early in her career, Claire took a sabbatical to serve in the Peace Corps. She spent five years in Nepal, helping to design and implement water-filtration and irrigation systems. Claire was academically gifted. She held several industrial-design patents in her name and had a knack for picking up languages. She charmed the locals by acquiring a functional aptitude for the Nepali language during her Peace Corps stay.

The back cover of her book included this summary:

I am beyond excited to share *To Live Is to Serve* with the world. I wrote this book to share how each of us has the power to change the world in our own way. Dreams do come true. A deep thank-you to ALL of the people on this planet who have supported me on my journey over the years. Thank you. Thank you. Thank you. This book and everything I have ever done, I did for you and because of you.

With all of my heart, Claire

The board was elated. They couldn't believe their good fortune at convincing someone as dynamic and talented as Claire to move to the small town of Summit City. Like everyone else, the organization had suffered through the pandemic of 2020, and the employees were struggling with remote work. The board decided they needed a dynamic leader who could be physically present four days a week to manage every detail and improve morale. The organization and the town were on the brink of a transformation. They wanted a strong leader who could bring them to the next stage of development.

Claire assured the board that being physically on-site would not be a problem. She insisted an on-site presence was critical to success. She noted how important it was to live amongst the people of Nepal when she was there during her service in the Peace Corps. Claire was warm and compassionate during the interviews. She was well-versed in the history of Summit City and the good works of Silver Creek Community Trust. She presented herself openly and humbly.

The board's hearts were full as they prepared to welcome Claire and help her move from her apartment on the Upper East Side of Manhattan to Summit City. Only one board member, John Williams, wasn't 100 percent convinced.

Claire captivated John just as she engaged the other board members, but something wasn't sitting right with him. When he tentatively suggested he wasn't sure, he received feedback from others that he might not be comfortable with a powerful woman.

John owned a manufacturing company that made ball bearings used in medical equipment, called Summit City Bearing Company. The company was located on the bank of the creek. John was the third generation of his family to own and operate Summit City Bearings. John and his family lived in the house his grandfather built, just a mile away from the plant. He was known as a practical businessman but was somewhat unpolished. The thought that he might not be able to interact with a powerful woman was something he would have to think about. He was questioning himself, wondering, "Am I intimidated by a powerful woman?" John continued to sit with the idea, however, he couldn't get over that something just wasn't quite right about Claire. She seemed too good to be true. She was overly warm. She listened too intently. He questioned why someone who'd lived such an exotic life would want to relocate to Summit City, Missouri. **John would later learn that Claire had no intention of moving to Summit City at all. She was saying what she needed to say to get the job. The Hogan Assessment identifies that those with the Leisurely personality type will appear to be friendly and cooperative while they are following their own agenda.**

There weren't many female leaders in Summit City. None came close to having the credentials of Claire Davis. One thing Claire did during the interview that didn't sit right with John was she kept reiterating that everyone could count on her for the "real truth." John thought, *Isn't the truth the truth? Why would she feel that it was necessary to clarify truth as being real?*

John also thought that Claire might be flirting with him. She laughed too easily, she threw her head back for emphasis after he made comments, and she gushed over his career and accomplishments. It didn't feel right to John, but he was reluctant to bring up the fact that she might be flirting with him. He wasn't sure it was true and didn't want to make such a serious allegation. **Claire was well aware that flirting would put John in a difficult position and would be impossible to prove.**

Other than the strange statement about the "real truth" and his concern about flirtatiousness, he thought everything about Claire was impressive. He admired her and hoped that his three daughters would be inspired by meeting someone so accomplished. He was excited about all she could bring and do for their community. He was hopeful she would bring some New York sophistication to Summit City.

CLAIRE DAVIS'S INTERVIEWS

Toxic leaders excel at impression management. They study what will be expected of them and do what they can to fulfill those expectations. Claire interviewed with the board via video conference. Claire was acutely aware that the board's endorsement would be key for her to get the position. She engaged them with worldly stories of Nepal, shared how her book dominated bestseller lists, and assured them that her presence in Summit City would result in increased revenue for the nonprofit and attract tourism to Summit City. The board was completely enamored, feeling Claire was a star. They could not believe their good fortune. **A common behavior with passive-aggressive behavior is overt positivity, making extreme promises, and telling people what they want to hear.**

While the board was enthralled with Claire, John Williams still wasn't convinced. He attempted to influence the other board members where he could. He suggested they keep interviewing to get a broader perspective and a larger pool of candidates. He was shot down with, "There's no time to waste!" John didn't feel comfortable mentioning that he perceived Claire was flirtatious, so he let it go. **When employees work with passive-aggressive leaders, they question themselves and their insights and examine their own behavior for flaws.**

John documented his perceptions of Claire but could not come up with a justifiable reason to avoid extending the offer. Soon Claire would be relocating to Summit City to accept the position of the CEO of Silver Creek Community Trust. John decided to bury his doubts and jump on-board to welcome Claire.

Claire sent thank-you notes to each board member written in calligraphy, including a brightly colored wax stamp of her initials on fine linen stationery. She gushed about the opportunity in her notes and reinforced her commitment to serving Silver Creek Community Trust. **Passive-aggressive leaders are often overly thoughtful, which can be very engaging to those they interact with. Their kindness will initially create strong trust environments.**

CLAIRE INTERACTS WITH DIRECT REPORTS AND MANAGERS

All went fine until Claire started her transition to Summit City, Missouri. SCCT had a staff of retired police officers who were retained to provide transportation services to senior leaders. These drivers were beloved in the small town of Summit City. Unfortunately, Claire, a world traveler and a New Yorker, underestimated the influence of her driver. She was also unaware of how interconnected people are in small towns.

Lenny was assigned as Claire's primary driver. He also golfed with John Williams. Their daughters roomed together in college, and their families knew each other well. After an enjoyable afternoon and eighteen holes of golf, John asked Lenny how it was going with Claire.

Lenny replied, "She's okay. Smart, always on time."

Hmmm. John probed, "Anything else? *On time* doesn't say much."

After a couple of beers, Lenny loosened up. He shared, "Well, I was kind of shocked that she didn't acknowledge me when she came to the car. She motioned for me to get her bags while she chatted away on her cell phone. I read her book, *To Live Is to Serve*. I was excited to meet her and expected someone who would be warm and welcoming. I guess she doesn't include drivers in the group of people who deserve to be served." **It's common for passive-aggressive leaders to dismiss those they perceive as not having power or unable to advance their own goals. Claire made the mistake of dismissing Lenny, John's friend and someone who was respected in the small town.**

John leaned back in his chair, looking puzzled. He replied, "Yes, I read her book, too. That *is* surprising." Now that Lenny felt free to express what he thought, he further shared, "Then I heard her on her cell phone. She was laughing loudly and saying that she couldn't believe she would be living in a town like Summit City. Then she whispered in a low tone, *"It won't be for long."* I thought she couldn't wait to move here. I was confused." John let it go at that but was starting to think he could be right about Claire and that she wasn't the person she projected herself to be. **Claire was starting to display passive-aggressive tendencies by saying one thing and doing another. She convinced the board that she was eager to move to Summit City. Now Lenny experienced another side of Claire, where she was sharing that her stay "wouldn't be for long."**

FRONT-LINE BEHAVIORS

Claire had five direct reports. Robert ran accounting, Lynne was responsible for human resources and legal counsel, Magda managed marketing, Anne was responsible for fundraising and development, and Leonard ran operations. Leonard was the son of Lenny, the company driver. After Leonard finished college at Iowa State, he returned home eager to work for Silver Creek Community Trust. His father, Lenny, had retired on disability after an accident when Leonard was a college freshman.

When Lenny was on the police force, he responded to a call to investigate a domestic dispute. The arguing couple lived in an older, framed house. As Lenny approached the front door, he crashed through the floorboards of the front porch. He needed extensive therapy to recover from the accident.

Leonard wanted to quit college and come home to help his father heal from the accident. Lenny wouldn't have it. He insisted that Leonard continue his education. Silver Creek Community Trust sponsored Lenny's education, with the understanding that he would come back and work for them for a few years. SCCT struggled with getting sophisticated talent. This solution seemed like a win-win for all.

Leonard worked at Summit City Bearing Company on his breaks from college. He learned about operations, earned an income, and was able to help at home. It wasn't easy for Leonard to work during his school breaks instead of relaxing or focusing on his studies. However, Leonard was willing to make the sacrifice because he thought it was the best solution for all involved.

During her first week on the job, Claire hosted a breakfast for her new team in a private banquet room at a local hotel. She greeted each leader as they walked in the door. The meeting was intended as a chance for them to begin forming a team.

Claire started the breakfast by stating, "This meeting is not about me, or even Silver Creek Community Trust. I want to know *how to make*

46

YOU successful." She added, "When I was in Nepal, we had a language barrier and were still able to implement an irrigation system. I'm sure we can do even more here." **Claire was already setting the stage that it won't be her fault if the team cannot accomplish goals. She announced she has experience producing results out of the country with the additional obstacle of language barriers. Very subtle to the untrained eye.**

Claire asked, "What does Silver Creek Community Trust need most?" Leonard replied, "Education-financing assistance." Claire took diligent notes. Robert added, "A more sophisticated operational software system would help. We also need a stronger cybersecurity defense against hackers. We were attacked and paid a ransom last year. If we didn't pay, the hackers would've shut us down. It wasn't worth the risk, so to our regret, we paid it." Claire scowled and continued to take notes. **Claire's frustration could be because these problems do not have easy fixes. She may feel that these challenges are out of her league. Feelings of inadequacy can manifest maladaptive actions in passive-aggressive leaders.**

Anne noted, "We have volunteers, but it seems we work more for them than they do for us. They are used to the legacy parties we throw for them and the gifts they receive. I feel like I do a lot of work keeping them happy, while we need a greater contribution." Claire nodded and continued to jot notes onto her tablet. Magda added, "I could save significant amounts of money by outsourcing the design and printing of our materials. However, we are tied to the community, and I must use local providers, especially since they are donors to SCCT." Claire nodded and then stated, "Lynne, we haven't heard from you. What type of support can legal use?" Lynne replied, "Well, all seems to be fine. However, I do have a concern that doesn't directly affect legal." Claire encouraged her by leaning forward, listening intently, and stating, "Please, go on."

Lynne shared, "Our 500 employees struggle with work/life balance. After the pandemic hit, many of them found themselves homeschooled in addition to working full-time at SCCT. Morale has been low. We need to find ways to continue to maximize the technology and resources we have while enhancing productivity."

"Agreed," Claire replied. She then snapped the cover of her tablet shut and started to end the meeting.

Leonard was confused. He asked, "Claire, don't you want to share what you need to succeed? Your ideas for SCCT? How can we support you?" Claire glared at Leonard for a minute. There was an uncomfortable silence. She slowly re-opened her tablet, leaned forward, and placed her elbows on the table. "Of course. How could I have neglected to share my expectations or what will be required to be successful?" *Leonard had unknowingly called Claire's bluff. He was sincere in his question. However, Claire did not have a plan. His question revealed that Claire was placing a significant amount of responsibility on the existing management to provide solutions. SCCT recruited Claire to bring fresh perspectives. He was eager to hear her ideas.*

Claire began to list her expectations. "First, always be open and honest with me. Share every detail, no matter how small or insignificant it may seem." **Asking for every detail to be shared is a way for Claire to control situations. If she knows everything that is going on, she can never be blindsided. She will continually create conditions where she will be successful and the star of the show.**

Claire went on, "In addition to our team meetings, I'd like to have regular monthly one-on-ones with you." *The individual meetings are another way for Claire to ensure she will never be surprised by any new information. The meetings are for her, not for the benefit of the manager, although, on the surface, one-on-one meetings seem to be a positive and productive activity.*

Claire concluded, "Lastly, don't feel like you need my permission to move forward with your plans and ideas. I'm here to serve you, empower you, and ensure you are successful. You are all intelligent people. There's no need to micromanage you. I'm here to remove roadblocks and barriers." Claire was greeted with big smiles from all around the table. The team was thrilled to have such a strong, sophisticated, supportive leader.

CLAIRE HOLDS A COMPANYWIDE TOWN HALL

Claire was concerned about the morale of SCCT's 500 employees. *Claire was aware that top leadership was blamed for poor morale and high turnover.* She decided the best way to approach it was to hold a town-hall meeting. She engaged the support of her personal assistant, Lucy, to manage all the details. Claire decided the meeting would be held via the company's electronic video-meeting program, and space would be made available for those who could attend in person.

Claire had a list of criteria she wanted Lucy to execute. The meeting should be fun and contain a Q&A session. Claire required that the employees submit their questions prior to the meeting. She wanted inspiring music playing in the background. Claire exclaimed to Lucy, "The meeting should be a five-star review; I want them to know that Claire Davis is in the house!"

Lucy was excited about having so much responsibility for preparing for the companywide town hall. She was concerned that the management team was not going to be involved. She approached Claire and asked, "Shouldn't we ask Robert, Lynne, Magda, Anne, and Leonard to take a section of the meeting?"

Claire smiled warmly at Lucy. "Great idea, Lucy! I love the way you have so many suggestions. It will take too much time to coordinate so many people for this meeting. I'd like to take this one on, and then we'll use your stellar idea and include them in the next one." Lucy was a little uncertain, so she asked, "Are you sure? It would be so much more productive if we included them. I know they'll have updates."

Claire smiled broadly again and stated, "I'm so glad to have your great brain on this team! We will include them next time for sure. This is just a little hello to the SCCT employees. No need to make a big thing out of it."

Just as Claire said it would be, the meeting was like a Broadway show! She had the crowd of employees on their feet—both at their home offices and in the corporate office—cheering at the company vision she painted, full of hope and possibility. Claire promised resources, answered carefully selected questions, and assured everyone all would be grand. Finally, she closed the meeting by stating that each employee would get a $500 cash bonus. This announcement was met with roaring praise.

UNPACKING THE TOWN-HALL MEETING

The following management meeting was held via conference call. Claire started the session with, "What's on your mind?" Robert stated, "I'll start. Where do you think we will get the $250,000 cash bonus you promised the employees?" Anne added, "Had I known, I could've gotten one of our patrons to donate funds. I have a list of people who want to give to causes they believe in." Lynne chimed in, "Some of the employees are on Performance Improvement Plans (PIPs). I'm hard-pressed to convince anyone that their performance is under par while they have $500 cash in their pocket. There's not an employment attorney in the land who will buy that. So, I guess we're stuck with them for another year or two." Magda added, "I could've helped with the meeting. I saw that you spent a fortune on the event. We are a nonprofit, you know." Leonard closed with, "We use those meetings to set operational expectations. It's a real missed opportunity. I'm not sure we can afford to have another companywide meeting anytime soon."

Claire feigned surprise. "I can't believe this! I'm so sorry. I thought I was doing the right, best thing for SCCT. I'm shocked Lucy didn't say anything during the planning. I guess I gave her too much responsibility. I thought she was ready for it. She helped me every step of the way. However, she obviously was not prepared to take on the role. I'm sorry—it's my fault for entrusting her with such an important task. I have much to learn about who I can count on." Claire put the meeting on mute and motioned as if she were calling Lucy. "Well, she's not here now. I don't quite know what to say. I can't be successful if I don't have a competent assistant. This is very disturbing. I'll handle this and get back to you at our next leadership meeting. I assure you this won't happen again."

Claire deflects responsibility by blaming Lucy, even though Lucy had suggested that she include the company managers. Lucy, an administrative assistant, doesn't have much power in the hierarchy. She also doesn't have the skills to deal with such extreme manipulation. Claire also offers a false apology. She appears to be taking responsibility by saying "I'm sorry," however, she is only sorry that someone else is not adequate. It's a slippery move. The managers feel heard but are unsure. They know Lucy, and she is not incompetent. She's also Leonard's wife, and the public thrashing infuriates him.

Claire was not aware that Lucy was Leonard's wife. He asked Lucy at dinner that night, "What happened at this company meeting? Why wasn't the senior leadership team involved?" Lucy stated, "I suggested that you be included, but Claire said she could handle it." Leonard looked shocked. "What??? She said that you told her not to include us." Upset, Lucy exclaimed, "That's not true! I asked her, and she said 'not this time' or something like that. Then she kept telling me how great I was."

Lucy was icy to Claire the next morning. Sensing something was wrong, Claire asked, "What's wrong, Lucy?" Lucy started to tear up. She was uncomfortable addressing the CEO of the company. She was a valued administrative assistant and did her best to do a great job.

Claire pulled up a chair next to Lucy's desk. She said, "Lucy, you can tell me the truth—*the real truth.* What's wrong?" Lucy started through stifled sobs, "I heard you told the managers that I suggested you handle the town-hall meeting independently, without their input." Claire sat back in her chair and exclaimed, "That's preposterous! I didn't say anything like that. In our last managers' meeting, I clearly told them how valuable you are and how I couldn't have pulled the meeting off without you. The problem is they just don't appreciate a leader like me, one who cares so much. They are not used to a hands-on leader. I'm here *to serve YOU*. I didn't move from *Manhattan* to do a bad job! I've put my heart and soul into this! I worked endless hours getting that meeting off the ground. I can't believe they don't appreciate me! I bet they are threatened. I don't see many powerful women in Summit City. Is this the kind of reception I will receive in this town?" **Claire denies what she said to the managers. Since it's a "he said/she said" situation, there is no hard proof of what she has done to Lucy and the managers. All of Claire's direct reports are now confused and feel they cannot perform adequately. And the toxic issue of lack of trust has been introduced into the culture.**

Lucy was now on the defensive, defending Claire, despite what she knew to be true—that Claire had manipulated her. "No!" Lucy exclaimed. "We are so happy to have you here. Didn't you see the article in the *Summit City Daily*? The town is gushing over you. I'm sure it was a misunderstanding on the managers' parts. It will get better as we go along. I hate to think you have a bad impression of us. We all want you to be successful." **Claire has successfully turned the situation around. At least the tactic is successful in her mind. She now has Lucy apologizing to her for her behavior. Lucy is questioning herself and defending Claire.** Lucy is a newly converted toxic enabler.

Claire sighed deeply. "Okay, Lucy. I don't know what I'd do without you. Don't forget, you can always count on the truth, the *real truth,* from me. In return, I'd like you to keep me informed of all the details of what's going on around here. No detail is too small. Why don't you take a day off, Lucy? It's a complimentary day. Just let me know when it will be. I want to thank you for all your hard work on the meeting." **Claire is using her suspicious catchphrase "the real truth." She also wants to make sure that Lucy keeps coming to her with information, so she can be prepared for anything that is thrown her way. Claire reinforces this by assuring Lucy "no detail is too small." Claire doles out another perk by giving Lucy a paid day off.**

CLAIRE DISAPPOINTS THE BOARD

The board depends on donations to fund essential programs, including child-care resources, advanced-education scholarships, travel opportunities, family support, and elder-care services. Claire assured the board during her interview that she would be able to recruit her worldwide network to fund the good work of SCCT. The donations are critical to the health of SCCT's programs. In addition, there are several notable businesses and families in Summit City that have the ability to donate.

Unfortunately, resources are tight for many. The board expressed their clear expectation that public appearances and presentations would be necessary to build relationships and secure donations. Claire volunteered that she would be able to raise funds not only locally but from her contacts around the country as well.

Claire was aware from her employment interviews that a contribution from one of their top philanthropists was up for renewal. She was informed that she would be expected to sponsor a dinner. Claire did not disclose that she despises these dinners, especially when she doesn't know anyone. However, during her interview, she convinced the board that she loves fundraising dinners and would be delighted to attend.

THE FUNDRAISING DINNER

Claire's assistant, Lucy, rented a historic mansion on the bank of Silver Creek to host the fundraising dinner. Chad Lewis, the philanthropist whose support was up for renewal, was attending. Claire was expected to attend and be the master of ceremonies at the intimate dinner. No expense was spared. Chad had recently been frustrated by the lack of leadership at SCCT and was wondering if his funds were being used effectively.

By now, the COVID-19 pandemic seemed to be under control. SCCT had taken every precaution possible to ensure the health and safety of their employees, program recipients, and donors. Although the threat of catching the virus was minimal, it was still possible to catch and transmit the highly contagious disease.

The morning of the event, Claire called the chair of the board, Peter Wilkinson, and stated, "Peter, I have awful news. I'm feeling terrible. I'm feverish, dizzy, and I keep coughing. I fear I have COVID. It would be irresponsible of me to attend the event. I don't want anyone to get sick." Peter was stunned. He was suspicious that Claire was not telling the truth. He had seen during her morning run on Silver Creek, and she appeared to be fine. Peter responded, "Claire, when did your symptoms start?" There was an uncomfortable silence on the line. Peter went on, "Mary Clark, the secretary of the board, is a physician. Please contact her to schedule an appointment so you can be tested." Claire replied, "Okay."

Claire had Lucy schedule an appointment for 2:30 p.m. in Dr. Mary Clark's office. Lucy knocked on Claire's door at 2:00 p.m. SCCT had a strong family environment. Lucy was aware of how vital Chad Lewis's donation would be for SCCT and the community they served. Lucy was also concerned for Claire's health and well-being. "Claire, I just wanted to remind you of your appointment with Dr. Clark."

Claire was on the phone and typing on her keyboard when Lucy entered her office. Claire nodded her acknowledgment. Lucy saw tissue boxes on Claire's desk and noticed her wastebasket was filled with wads of used tissues. Claire was coughing loudly and wiping her eyes. Finally, she gathered her bag, a handful of tissues, and through pained coughs, said, "See you at the mansion."

2:30 came and went. Claire did not show up at Dr. Clark's office. At 4:00 p.m., Claire called Peter and said, "Peter, I just woke up. I'm feeling awful. I was so dizzy driving, I thought it would be safer to come straight home. No one knows how severe this virus is or how many people can be affected. I cannot, in good conscience, attend the event." Claire ended the call. Peter was stunned. *Claire passive-aggressively used everyone's knowledge of the pandemic to keep from attending.*

Claire has left Silver Creek Community Trust in a quandary. COVID-19 was a contagious disease. On the surface, it appeared Claire was being responsible. However, her passive-aggressive behaviors toward many individuals, including board members, revealed there could be more going on in this situation.

At this point, the board was considering releasing Claire, which could result in a drawn-out and expensive lawsuit. In addition, they would still need to find a replacement for Claire. With the toxic culture being supported by the board by allowing Claire to remain in leadership, the team started to lose productivity as employees started taking sick days, show up late for meetings, and create their own plausible excuses for avoiding difficult situations. Morale begin to plummet while people blamed themselves for the shortcomings of SCCT. This is a classic toxic situation that required a trained professional to intervene.

The next section covers borderline personality disorder. As we continue to outline common personality disorders that afflict senior leaders, I will provide tools to identify the disorders and alternative solutions that can create a positive work environment with productive individuals throughout the organization.

Borderline Personality Disorder

THE WORD "BORDERLINE" APTLY DESCRIBES the traits of this personality. A person with this disorder is often highly functional. They generally have a deep need for intimacy and connection but, paradoxically, engage in behaviors that push people away. Their constant behavioral push and pull is exhausting for everyone around them. They often suffer silently with their affliction because borderline personality disorder masks deep, unmet emotional needs.

Common characteristics of borderline personality disorder (BPD) are severe mood swings, impulsive behavior, and difficulty establishing and maintaining stable personal relationships. With a borderline personality, you never know what you are going to get. Behavior can change from day to day or even within the same day.

It might seem like the person with borderline personality disorder has a large circle of friends. In reality, they have connections, but they do not have relationships where both parties are vulnerable and are equal partners. Those with BPD are *takers*—they do not know how to give. They are often the life of the party and may be captured smiling, having the time of their lives, in every photo opportunity. They let others come close—and then pull away. They will sabotage relationships, divide teams, and protect their position at all costs.

Leaders with borderline personality disorder may have a string of marriages and divorces, and they are often not on speaking terms with their children or families. They will always have a reason to explain why these relationships are damaged. They might blame their former marriage partner for turning the children against them. They will accuse their marriage partner of infidelity, stealing money, or having ulterior motives in the relationship. A person with BPD will never be at fault. Whatever happens, happens **to them**. They are always an innocent victim of circumstance. They will be the hero or the victim in any story they tell. The person with BPD will not assume responsibility. They do not question what they can do to make situations better. If they ever do apologize for their behavior or a situation, it will be followed with claims of *"You made me do it,"* or *"I had no choice."* However, if all goes well, they will take all the credit. This might sound similar to a narcissist, and it is. People generally do not have just one personality disorder. They can exhibit several disorders with varying degrees of severity.

Interacting with people who have borderline personality disorder can be very confusing because their behavior is *just on the border* of what is acceptable. Since their behavior is usually within acceptable boundaries, they might justify any of their extreme behaviors based on specific situations and current cultural norms. Senior leaders generally have a great deal of talent that counterbalances their flaws.

Those with BPD frequently display addictive behaviors. The addictions can include eating, gambling, legal or illegal drug use, sex, workaholism, exercising, obsessive attention to social media, watching sports, participating in extreme sports, or any other behavior carried to the point of excess. Women are more likely than men to be diagnosed with BPD. One reason is that women tend to seek therapy and treatment more frequently than men, so more data is available. In addition, cultural norms make more allowances for men's erratic behavior. A woman will more easily experience criticism for mood swings, for example, than a man will. If a woman appears to be "out of control," she is characterized as "moody." However, if a man displays bursts of anger or demands to be left alone, he is sometimes even admired by friends and coworkers for his strength of character.

This double standard often applies to a range of behaviors. If a man drinks too much at company meetings, gambles excessively, or displays characteristics of sex addiction, those around him may tend to minimize his behavior. You have probably heard managers and coworkers say, "Oh, that's just Charlie being Charlie." Research data suggests these are symptoms of something more serious, such as borderline personality disorder, a leadership derailer. It is worth noting that women, on the other hand, are often held to a higher, less-forgiving standard, especially where sexual behavior is concerned.

Because the symptoms are treatable, we have access to a great deal of information on borderline personality disorder from the work done by treatment centers and programs for substance abuse and addictive behaviors. The person with BPD may do very well in treatment, so the therapy will appear to have been successful. However, treating the symptoms is a temporary solution that does not address the root of the disorder. The craving for intimacy, appreciation, recognition for who they are, just as they are, outside of their accomplishments, remains unsatisfied. Consequently, even after treatment, people with BPD can be at risk for suicide or self-harm, including a behavior known as "cutting." Cutting is when a person creates small wounds across their body. Inflicting pain enables them to feel something, rather than not experiencing any sensation or emotion at all. When the symptoms are treated but the core disorder is not addressed, the leader with BPD may exchange one maladaptive behavior for another.

In this section, I will share three case studies derived from my practice with senior leaders who exhibited symptoms of borderline personality disorder. The people most impacted by the leader with BPD are generally direct reports, who often hold very high positions themselves but are unprotected from the erratic behaviors of their more senior manager.

As we will see in these cases, leaders with BPD are very adept at covering their tracks. They have developed a system of protection by positioning themselves as central to the organization, its infrastructure, and its future success. I've mentioned that narcissistic, passive-aggressive, and borderline qualities often present in one individual simultaneously. Our first case study demonstrates how this might manifest itself in an especially toxic and damaging combination of behaviors.

Case Study 1: AI Robotics

LILY, WHO WE FIRST ENCOUNTERED in the narcissistic personality disorder discussion in Section II, was a managing partner of AI Robotics. Lily displayed narcissistic behavior by always making sure she was squarely in the limelight, where she received the constant recognition that she felt entitled to. But her constant need for risk and excitement were consistent with borderline personality disorder behaviors as well. Her actions, such as creating a team-building exercise that required her employees to jump out of a plane, showed how her disorder shaped her decisions. She liked to boast about her extreme sports activities and often referred to herself as "Supergirl" and "a real thrill seeker."

Imposing Lily's erratic behavior on AI Robotics employees caused high turnover and made recruiting top talent even more difficult. Employees simply could not meet her expectations for risk-taking, and many grew tired of her tendency to take all the credit for everyone else's hard work. Management-team members Chad and Taylor finally agreed with their partner Gary that Lily and AI Robotics had to part ways. One factor that influenced their decision was that AI Robotics was a takeover target. If AI Robotics received a lucrative buyout, Chad and Taylor, as founding partners, would profit substantially from the sale of their start-up. While Chad and Taylor liked and even admired Lily, the employee turnover she caused—along with the subsequent lower company performance—hurt their prospects of finding a top buyer. This case study depicts what happened when Gary, as chief human-resources officer, gave Lily the bad news of their decision to terminate her position.

Gary began the termination process by asking Lily to meet with him in person. His phone rang precisely at the moment the meeting was scheduled to start. It was Lily, via video call. She appeared to be in a hospital bed with her leg elevated. Gary opened by asking with genuine concern, "Hi, Lily. What *happened*?" Lily responded with a big smile, saying, "Remember I told you about the trek I was taking in the Amazon and how challenging it was going to be? Well, even though I'm in excellent shape, I had a slight slip. The doctor thought it would require emergency surgery, but I was able to avoid that." Lily continued, "I've been having some undiagnosed abdominal pain for the past four days, though. The doctors think it is most likely a muscular-skeletal issue. They've ordered me to stay on bed rest for two weeks to see if it helps."

Gary stared blankly into the video screen. He'd heard these kinds of stories from Lily before—the time she "ate something weird" and had to undergo tests and treatment for days, or the time she had a mysterious shooting pain in her right arm that made it impossible for her to work, even though they had an important deadline to meet. Her stories didn't ever add up or make sense. And there were never any actual medical records or corroborating information from her so-called doctors. As he tried to decide how to respond, Gary thought, *I'm so tired of playing this game. What is a muscular-skeletal issue? Is it muscular, or is it skeletal? What does abdominal pain have to do with anything?* Two-week hospital stays were highly unusual, especially for something that wasn't serious. If Lily had not already had a history of grand stories, Gary might have believed her. However, Lily's long and consistent pattern of dramatic fabrications made Gary doubt her tale.

Finally, Gary replied, "I'm very sorry about your situation, Lily. I was hoping we could chat in person. But unfortunately, this conversation can't wait for another two weeks." As if to underscore her situation, Lily smiled while jiggling her elevated leg for emphasis. "Of course, Gary. What's on your mind?"

Gary held some documents in front of the screen so Lily could view them. "Lily, I'm looking at the notes from our previous conversations. In those talks we discussed how your performance, especially the problem you've had retaining good employees, has compromised our ability to find a qualified buyer for AI Robotics. I hope the reason for today's meeting is not a surprise. We need a more-consistent leadership team to move a potential sale forward. Chad and Taylor are the right leaders for AI at this critical time. We can't afford to lose another prospective buyer. Our last deal fell through with Vega Automation because they were concerned about risk, operational inconsistency, and AI Robotics' high insurance costs. All of these factors can be traced back to poor employee retention. As cofounders, Chad and Taylor have decided that it's best to part ways with you, Lily. With Chad and Taylor as the senior leadership, AI Robotics will be a more-attractive company. I'm sorry it had to come to this, but we want to make a clean and fair separation. I have prepared your severance agreement. Please let me know where we can send your severance package."

Now it was Lily's turn to stare blankly into the screen. She turned away slightly from the camera, but Gary saw the tears streaming down her face. Silently Gary questioned how real the tears were. Lily had frequently been very dramatic, acting out highs and lows over their years as co-workers. Gary had hoped that, in her role as managing partner, Lily would recognize she had a responsibility to do what was best for the stability and future of the firm.

After a long, painful silence, Lily finally spoke angrily. "I can't believe you would do this to me! After all I've done for you. I've covered up your incompetence. I've provided exemplary leadership to AI Robotics. Everyone there loves me. Obviously, it's you who has a problem. You have an issue with powerful women." She ended the video call abruptly, leaving Gary unsure of what her next move would be.

LILY MOVES INTO ACTION

Lily decided to go on the offensive and try to reactivate the deal by calling Adam Caldwell, CEO of Vega Automation. "Adam! I'm glad I caught you. I wanted to share an idea I have for AI Robotics, something I discovered while hiking in the Amazon last week. My idea will propel AI Robotics to even greater heights. I need to meet with you as soon as possible." Adam was intrigued enough to agree to a meeting. Lily then contacted the two employees she'd gone skydiving with, René and Patrick. She texted them to arrange a quick conference call, telling them they needed to contact her because she had a lucrative opportunity for them to review. The call began, "René! Patrick! I have big news: Vega Automation is set to buy AI Robotics. YES, it's true! I need you both on my team to help us get through the transition. Can I count on you?" René and Patrick were thrilled at the potential career prospects of this new opportunity. They agreed they would support Lily.

THE NEWS GETS BACK TO CHAD AND TAYLOR

Meanwhile Chad received a call from AI Robotics' investment banker, Joelle Garcia. She started the call by saying, "Vega Automation has stalled negotiations until they speak to Lily." Chad was shocked. "What? There must be some mistake. We've just offered Lily a separation package. Vega Automation said they were uncomfortable working with her." Joelle explained, "She called Adam Caldwell, stating she wanted to share a new idea with him. He was intrigued enough to listen. Unfortunately, the deal has stalled."

Chad ended the call, shaking his head and bewildered by this turn of events. When he called Taylor, he discovered Taylor had already heard the disturbing news. "René and Patrick emailed me to thank me for the new opportunity Lily promised them," Taylor reported. Chad, now exasperated, said, "Let's get Gary involved. We need to do some damage control. Who knows what Lily is telling people."

ORGANIZATIONAL REPERCUSSIONS

Given her past borderline personality disorder behavior of seizing the spotlight, claiming the credit, dramatizing events, and demanding recognition, Lily's performance should not have taken Gary, Chad, and Taylor by surprise. Unfortunately, they expected Lily to act in the best interest of the entire organization. Instead, she would always do the thing that is *best for her*, even when it involves lying and manipulating others.

Despite his concerns about Lily and the complaints he made to Chad and Taylor about her, Adam Caldwell didn't want to miss a big opportunity; after all, bottom-line results win. He was willing to communicate with Lily, mistakenly thinking she might be the brains behind the whole operation. Meanwhile, Gary struggled with trying to lead through influence. He did not have direct control over Chad and Taylor's actions. All he could do was suggest solutions. Chad and Taylor were so excited about the growth potential of AI Robotics, they were okay taking shortcuts to get things done. Now the fragile structure of AI Robotics was beginning to implode. If the company succeeded, it would be by accident, not based on sound strategy and policies, employees, vendors, contractors, or anything anyone who interacted with AI Robotics could rely on. It was unfortunate because there was genuine potential at AI Robotics that could not be fully realized without putting in place clearly established systems and consistently enforcing them.

Behavioral and Clinical Insights

Since Lily's behavior has been tolerated for so long, it makes it difficult to draw the line that she had finally gone too far. Her excessive behavior and unreliable reputation are apparent only to insiders at AI Robotics. Lily chose to go outside the company for exactly this reason, to make herself important to the potential buyer.

AI Robotics is operating in a state of chaos and may never recover. After several buyers declined the opportunity to purchase the firm, they are beginning to develop a reputation as a bad investment. The employees are not aligned with the organizational objectives. No one is clear on what to do, their authority, or who is in charge. René and Patrick are chasing an opportunity they think will be lucrative and glamorous. Their history with Lily makes them think she might have some good ideas, and they should take the risk and follow her. As is commonly the case with borderline personality disorder leaders, Lily has used her considerable verbal skills to win allies, convince them to view her as a victim of underperforming direct reports, and make them believe she brings great value to the company.

Case Study II: Relay Fulfillment Center

MARYLYN JACKSON, CEO of Relay Fulfillment Center, Inc., had recently hired Thomas Dodson as SVP of global call-center operations. Relay Fulfillment Center's slogan was "Count on Us!" Relay prided itself on the fact that any customer who called received a response within five minutes. As a result, Relay attracted a demanding clientele and was able to charge a premium for their personalized service while enjoying a profitable niche in the marketplace. Marylyn had recently been promoted to CEO. She previously had held the SVP role and was directly involved in recruiting Thomas as her replacement as SVP.

Thomas reported to Marylyn's office to begin his new role. He was struck by how impressive her office was, with floor-to-ceiling windows, a desk in the center, and a corner receiving area furnished with a small table and two chairs. Warm colors and many pictures of Marylyn's adult son, his children, and her standard poodle, Pearl, helped to personalize the inviting space.

THOMAS'S FIRST DAY

Although Thomas arrived at 8:00 a.m., Marylyn informed him she had been at the office since 6:00 a.m. Marylyn's two driving forces were physical fitness and a commitment to work. She was very proud that she was able to raise a son while rising through the executive ranks of a competitive business environment. Marylyn attributed her personal and professional success to her relentless drive and determination to always find a way to get things done.

Marylyn greeted Thomas with a hearty "Hello" but then surprised him with a hug. Immediately uncomfortable, Thomas stiffened and stepped back. "Come, come," she urged, motioning to the small table in the corner nook. "Sit," she commanded with a big smile. Thomas sat straight-backed, without settling deeper into the chair. "Thomas," Marylyn cooed, "we are so happy you accepted the position. We at Relay know you will accomplish great things."

Thomas carefully responded in a neutral tone, "I intend to do all I can, Marylyn."

She slapped the table energetically. "Great! So, what can I do to ensure your success?"

Thomas was uncertain how to proceed. "Well, I haven't met the team yet or assessed the records. I'm not sure of the baseline of personnel performance or the state of current operations. Maybe we can start there. That might give me a better idea of how you may be able to help me."

Marylyn seemed disappointed but conceded, "Of course. You need to get settled in."

To Thomas, her response felt like condescension, but since he did not know her well, he shrugged her comment off.

Marylyn added, "I know this is personal, but I want to assure you that you have my full support. I understand that you suffer from multiple sclerosis. We are a family-oriented company, and I want to promise you, you will have all you need."

Thomas took a moment before he replied. "Marylyn, I'm a little surprised you brought this up. While there's nothing that I need, I would like to share a constructive criticism, if I may. I'm not comfortable with the word 'suffer.' It's true I have a chronic illness, and I manage the symptoms. 'Suffering' is not how I describe my situation."

Marylyn responded stiffly, with a fixed smile, "Of course. I understand completely!"

Thomas continued, "I generally don't disclose this information unless there is a business requirement to do so. I trust that you will keep details about my health confidential."

Marylyn kept a smile on her face but did not respond. Thomas accepted her smiling silence as acknowledgment that he could trust her to keep his health private.

As Marylyn stood to move back behind her imposing desk, she signaled a shift in power and the end of the two-way dialogue. "Well, Thomas, we have our launch meeting on Monday. At that time, we will introduce you to the global call-center team. Some members will be in person; others will call in remotely. I want to make it clear that this is your show. You should use this meeting to set expectations and discuss how you want the global call center to run. During the last several years, staff members have been working remotely, with flexible hours. We've established that how they get the work done is unimportant. The essential performance factor is that all inquiries receive a response within five minutes. It can be via a phone call, text message, instant message, or email. It's your job to continue to meet that metric." Marylyn winked. "Pretty simple, huh?"

Thomas once again was unsure how to respond to her joking, conspiratorial manner.

She closed their first meeting with a dismissal. "Well, Thomas, I've taken up too much of your valuable time. I'm sure you want to prepare for the launch meeting. Please plan to meet with me thirty minutes prior to the meeting, so I understand how to best support you in this session."

At dinner with his wife, Layla, Thomas shared the details of his puzzling first day. "Layla, it was all a little odd. I couldn't believe she brought up the MS. I thought those records were confidential. I disclosed the information only to HR. She also had this frozen smile, which never seemed to move. Her office looked like a family room. It wasn't very businesslike at all."

"Well," Layla said, "it's your first day. You can't make all these assessments in one day. I'm sure she's fine. Just do what you know how to do, and you'll be great."

Thomas felt reassured. "I guess you're right. I'll just get down to looking at the operations and not think about the rest."

Layla agreed. "Now you're talking. This is all brand-new; you have to look at it with fresh eyes."

THE DAY OF THE LAUNCH MEETING

As requested, Thomas arrived at Marylyn's office thirty minutes early. He didn't want to risk being late. Marylyn looked commanding in a power outfit of a navy-blue suit with a skirt, matching pumps, a white blouse, and a gold choker necklace. This was distinctly different from the relaxed dress code and vibe at Relay Call Center, especially now that most people were working remotely. Thomas had deliberately chosen to dress business casual to reinforce that informal attire was acceptable, even at the highest levels of management.

Marylyn remarked on his clothes. "Thomas, I'm so glad you wore the company T-shirt! Perfect. You want the employees to think you are one of them. Okay, let's get down to it. What do you have prepared?"

Once again, her tone struck Thomas as mocking or condescending. He set aside his feelings about the T-shirt remark and dove into his plans for the meeting.

Thomas led with good news. "Well, I've run the numbers, and I'm pleased to report they are quite good. Even though most of the workforce is remote, we respond to inquiries within the five-minute time frame 90 percent of the time."

Marylyn's frozen smile accompanied a quick nod and her curt reply, "Go on."

Thomas continued, "Furthermore, the last company survey depicts that 70 percent of the employees are 'very satisfied' with their environment."

Marylyn shot back, with her frozen smile, "So, what's your plan?"

Thomas went on, "Well, since remote is now the way of the world, and we manage so many different time zones, my plan is to integrate this flexibility into our daily operations. I plan to share how well we've been doing so the employees can feel recognized as a big part of our success.

"I also plan to share a feedback system I've developed. The idea is to capture all employees' suggestions so we can continue to evolve and grow as a company. We made so many strides when the pandemic of 2020 hit. However, those enhancements were reactive. My thought is we can capture the potential of suggestions to be *proactive* with growth and change. This strategy will create sustainable growth for Relay."

He expected a response from Marylyn, but all she added was a distracted, "Okay, let's get to it."

THE MEETING BEGINS

Marylyn entered the meeting room ahead of Thomas. Employees were scattered throughout the auditorium-style room, with one or two empty chairs between them for increased health safety. Screens connecting the remote workforce were installed around the room. Employees participating remotely had not been required to have their cameras on, so while some staff were visible, others were not. The globally dispersed workforce was checking in from many different time zones. It was 9:00 a.m. in Cleveland, Ohio, 6:30 p.m. in India, 1:00 a.m. in Russia, 7:00 a.m. in California, and 8:00 p.m. in China. Many of the employees in Ohio chose to attend the meeting from their home offices rather than return to the office. This meeting was mandatory, and it appeared that every employee had made a special effort to attend. The thousands of people on the call were eager to meet Thomas and hear what he, as their new SVP, had to say.

Marylyn addressed the employees from a podium and exclaimed, "Welcome! I must tell you how grateful we are at Relay for your exceptional performance in the most trying of circumstances. Even with illness, homeschooling, and caring for family members, you have been able to meet the metric of answering the majority of inquiries within a five-minute timeframe. We are grateful." Marylyn continued, "It's a very different day today. When I had my son, John, I called in from the hospital bed to check my voicemails hours after his birth. Today, as I look out into this auditorium, I see empty seats. It was too difficult for many to come in. We are a global company and must remain competitive. Thomas Dodson, our new SVP of global operations, is also a man who achieves. Even though he *manages* a chronic illness, he never lets it affect his performance. I'm pleased to introduce you to Thomas Dodson."

Thomas was shocked on many levels. He wasn't sure what had just happened. Marylyn had derailed his entire plan. She'd made a negative remark about absent employees that set the wrong tone for his positive and congratulatory remarks. His whole plan was based on praising efficiency and employee input. Marylyn undermined his positive message and further diminished him by disclosing his illness to the employees. Her assertions ensured that everyone knew that she was still the leader running the show. She used Thomas's illness to reinforce her power as the person who was really in charge. She essentially cast a shadow of doubt on Thomas's ability to lead from day one.

Disconcerted and upset by this breach of trust, Thomas muddled through the information he wanted to share. This wasn't at all what he'd expected to happen or what he had carefully planned for. He fumbled through his presentation and ended the meeting by informing the employees he planned to continue to seek their input on creating a positive work environment at Relay.

AFTER THE MEETING

Thomas marched straight to Marylyn's office without making an appointment. He worked to control his anger and hurt but needed to let Marylyn know how disappointed he was. To his amazement, Marylyn wrapped Thomas in a big hug and exclaimed, "Thomas, you were *wonderful!*"

Thomas broke out of the unwanted hug, uncomfortable with the physical contact. "Marylyn, I'm not sure what happened in there."

Marylyn glared at him. "What do you mean, 'what happened'? We reported that, by and large, employees are meeting metrics of answering requests within five minutes."

Thomas, uninvited, sank into a chair with his elbows on his knees and his hands clasped together. "I was surprised by your introduction. I thought in our pre-meeting, we agreed that you would turn the meeting over to me. Instead, your comments undermined the points I wanted to make, including that everyone was doing a great job. Had the meeting gone as I thought we had decided, I would have shared some specific ideas to build upon Relay's current success. Even more disturbing to me, there was no reason to share confidential information about my health."

Marylyn looked shocked. She screamed, *"Undermined??* You have an opportunity to lead a global team. I had to claw my way up the corporate ladder to earn opportunities like this. You just *waltz in* and expect everything handed to you."

Thomas was stunned. Her erratic behavior unnerved him. One minute she was hugging him and smiling, and, the next, she was screaming and insulting him. This is a common response to people who unpredictably overreact. Instead of questioning the person, their behavior prompts the listener to back off. Given the way the conversation was going, Thomas felt that now was not the time to address the broken confidence, the self-serving comments about checking her voicemails after giving birth, or the other ways she prevented him from making the strong and positive impression he had planned to foster in the global meeting.

Rather than continue with a confrontation, Thomas decided to back down. "Marylyn, ours is a new working relationship. I clearly misunderstood and did not plan for this meeting appropriately." He left her office knowing there was no reason for him to accept blame, but feeling he had no other way to respond to this situation.

ORGANIZATIONAL REPERCUSSIONS

For the first time since the beginning of 2020, Relay missed its five-minute response time metric the next day. Employees were confused and disheartened by the all-employee meeting. They used the company chat system in high volume, venting that they felt unappreciated for all they had done to mobilize Relay during a crisis brought about by the COVID-19 global pandemic. Instead of answering company inquiries, they poured their energy into communicating with each other. Their distress and confusion led many to question whether Thomas had the ability to lead Relay into the future.

Employees who were not venting their frustrations were updating their resumes and visiting job boards. They felt betrayed. Others felt undervalued and justified in prioritizing their personal responsibilities for taking care of children and elderly parents rather than attempting to focus only on creating success for Relay.

Some employees continued conducting business as usual, but they were affected by the disengagement of their peers. The company was in a state of turmoil. Marylyn was outraged that Relay failed their five-minute response metric so soon under Thomas's leadership. Marylyn demanded that Thomas meet with her the next morning. Thomas had a long-scheduled appointment with a neurologist who was nearly impossible to see. Thomas asked if he could meet Marylyn in the afternoon. Marylyn responded by questioning his dedication to his new job. Thomas canceled his appointment, risking his health, to attend the meeting with Marylyn.

Marylyn was dressed in her workout clothes. As usual, she had been at the office for hours when Thomas walked in at 8:00 a.m., and it was obvious she had been working out. Since she was dressed so formally before, Thomas had decided that he should wear a pressed shirt, a sport coat, and slacks for this meeting.

Marylyn did not invite Thomas to sit down. She launched right into what felt like an interrogation. "Thomas, what happened? Things were going so well at Relay, but, after your presentation at the companywide, things suddenly just fell apart."

Thomas took a deep breath. "Well, I'm wondering the same thing. We reviewed the plan I had prepared to address the employees, but the plan seemed to go wrong when the meeting started."

Marylyn shot back, "What do you mean, *go wrong?*"

Thomas carefully chose his words. "I did not get to present the plan we agreed on."

Marylyn shouted, "Are you implying this catastrophe of service is *my fault?* You've been on-board for *two days*, and Relay is out of control. Clients are complaining, and employees are not focused. I thought you could handle this!"

Thomas attempted to sputter out a defense—"I tried"—before Marylyn cut him off. "Thomas, you're fired. We have a ninety-day trial period at Relay, and I can't risk eighty-eight more days with you."

Behavioral and Clinical Insights

The borderline behaviors Marylyn displays in this situation are inappropriate physical contact, breaching trust, deliberately putting an employee at a disadvantage to strengthen her own image, and reacting with outrage when held accountable for her damaging actions.

Leaders in the CEO position are generally very polished presenters, capable of fostering an impression of command and confidence in front of large audiences. However, behind closed doors, it's commonly an entirely different story. Leaders like Thomas are often equally talented at presenting and communicating to large groups of people. Many times, they will endure the leader's undermining behavior and attempt to deal with it privately or tolerate it, putting the good of the organization ahead of their individual needs.

Thomas's situation is precarious. Since Marylyn did not support him in the onboarding process in his new role as SVP, it might appear that Thomas was not qualified for the role. The only two people who know what happened are Thomas and Marylyn. Marylyn has a long-standing history of success. However, she did not create an environment where Thomas could be successful. Relay will now be in a position to seek Thomas's replacement. Marylyn stands to, once again, come out as the hero who saved the day. She will either find someone she can fully control and feels comfortable with—or she will repeat the experience with the next leader. Marylyn knows enough about the company to salvage its operations.

Many leaders like Marylyn stay in their positions for years. There's an old joke that leaders like Marylyn hire someone new to run with the "ball of progress," and then make sure they are tackled at every opportunity. Marylyn is savvy. She operates close to the line of what is acceptable and pulls back or pushes forward at just the right time. Her obsessions are fitness and work, which go undetected as addictions. Productivity and a commitment to health are valued in many organizations, so extreme commitment to these behaviors is admired and revered.

Case Study III: NOVO Bio-Organics

NOVO BIO-ORGANICS was a spinoff company of a Fortune 500 pharmaceutical company. The company created immune-building drugs from bio-organic material in the sea, including seaweed and coral. This aggressive and creative project had been bleeding research funds for decades, with no clear indication of when it might turn a profit. So, when a team of scientists offered to buy NOVO Bio-Organics, the parent company easily agreed, confident that, while using bio-organic material as a drug source held promise, it would never be realized or commercialized in any of their lifetimes.

The scientists who acquired the company, Dr. Rob Ogden, Dr. Celia Hamid, and Dr. Viral Raj, were elated with their good fortune. Full of enthusiasm and unsuspecting of any barriers, they sought funding for the development of organic drugs. They were confident material that flourished in the ocean could create healing possibilities that seemed limitless.

THE TEAM ATTENDS THEIR FIRST VENTURE-CAPITAL MEETING

Dr. Raj had a contact from his days at the Massachusetts Institute of Technology (MIT). Based on his relationship, he was able to negotiate a meeting with Accelerator, a venture-capital firm known for gambling on big ideas—and winning. The NOVO Bio-Organic team was overwhelmed with dreams of the possibilities funding could provide. From their base in Philadelphia, they flew first-class to California, confident they were going to close a big deal. Although people were still skittish about air travel after the COVID-19 pandemic, the team felt the meeting was so critical that their ideas needed to be presented in person. As they walked into Accelerator's office, Dr. Raj noticed that Dr. Ogden's shirt was untucked. He grabbed him by the back of his belt, startling Dr. Ogden, and pushed his shirt into his pants. Dr. Ogden was stunned. Dr. Hamid smirked a little, incredulous at what she had just witnessed. She'd seen Dr. Raj behave oddly before and dismissed it. He was obsessed with his appearance. He was equally adamant about constantly being accessible. They joked that he answered the phone in the shower. However, each of these professionals was highly educated and experienced in working on high-stakes projects. They good-naturedly tolerated each other's eccentricities. As a result, behavior that might seem intolerable to others was sometimes overlooked.

THE INVESTMENT MEETING

Dr. Raj kicked off the meeting by warmly stating, "It is my distinct pleasure to introduce you to my esteemed colleagues, Dr. Cecilia Hamid and Dr. Rob Ogden. One is rarely fortunate enough to be graced with such brilliance." He continued speaking without leaving space for even a word from his colleagues. Violating rule number one of professional presentations, Dr. Raj had placed his phone on the table. He glanced at the light flashing on his phone while he talked, continually breaking eye contact with the audience. He thought he was being discreet, but his behavior distracted everyone in the room.

He began laying out the qualifications of his fellow scientists. "Dr. Hamid first noticed the healing properties of coral while diving in Guam during her time in the Peace Corps. She took a gap year after earning her PhD from Harvard." His phone continued to flash. Dr. Raj finally turned the phone over while he continued to speak. "Dr. Ogden is an award-winning research scientist. I spend a good deal of my time warding off other firms that attempt to steal him!"

Dr. Raj painted a vision of how the healing properties of coral and seaweed would change the lives of many, even entire nations, for the greater good of all by creating stronger immune systems that would minimize the risk of viral infection. He was an excellent presenter, but his partners began to realize Dr. Raj was departing from the script they had practiced in Philadelphia. Dr. Ogden and Dr. Hamid were supposed to play key speaking roles in the presentation. Instead, they sat waiting to be called upon while Dr. Raj dominated the show.

The pitch was well received. The team left Accelerator with promises from management that they would be in touch.

AFTER THE MEETING

The team of scientists headed to the airport, pleased with the positive response from Accelerator. Even though Dr. Raj had shut them out, Dr. Hamid and Dr. Ogden were able to swallow their disappointment because it appeared they might get the funding. However, Dr. Ogden was still upset by Dr. Raj grabbing him and tucking in his shirt. It was humiliating. Dr. Hamid and Dr. Ogden were both irritated by Dr. Raj's attention to his cell phone during the presentation, especially since this was something they had spoken to him about many times before.

The team headed to the airport lounge to unwind until it was time for their return flight to Philadelphia. Dr. Raj grabbed a bunch of candy bars and ordered a gin martini. Dr. Hamid ordered fruit juice, and Dr. Ogden ordered a carrot juice.

Once they were seated in the lounge, Dr. Ogden addressed Dr. Raj's odd behavior. "Raj, what was that about? I'm walking into a meeting, and you treat me like a child. I can tuck my own shirt in." Dr. Raj waved the server down, ready for his second martini. Dr. Ogden and Dr. Hamid still had their juices. Only minutes had passed, and already Dr. Raj was on his second cocktail.

Dr. Hamid chimed in, "And you *promised* to leave your cell phone in the car!"

Dr. Raj, outraged, first directed his comments to Dr. Ogden: "You looked like an idiot! These are my colleagues from MIT! I *saved* you; I *rescued* the meeting. Neither one of you said anything! If it wasn't for me, this project would be in a ditch. The parent company didn't sell it for no reason. It needs *work*."

Dr. Raj continued, "I have to admit that the two of you are beginning to look like dead weight. These are *my* contacts; you two are nothing without me. There is no way you could've gotten this meeting without me. Neither of you said a word during the whole pitch, leaving me to figure it all out. Do you know how much I have risked for this opportunity?" He downed the rest of his martini and flagged the server for a third.

Dr. Hamid thought Dr. Raj might need some water after consuming so much alcohol so quickly. She motioned for the server to fill their water glasses. She found Dr. Raj's behavior perplexing. It was Raj who dominated the meeting and didn't give them an opportunity to speak at all. Even though the meeting did not go as they had practiced, she thought it went well. She said, "Raj, I had no idea. I thought you *wanted* to lead the meeting. Had I known, I would've stepped up, but you were amazing, and I thought we were supporting you." She paused, full of remorse, and added, "I'm sorry if you feel we let you down."

Dr. Ogden, still feeling disrespected and slighted by the shirt incident, didn't think an apology was necessary. He spoke up. "Dr. Hamid, Raj is being a jerk. No need to apologize to him."

Dr. Hamid spoke soothingly to try to calm things down. "Raj has worked so hard for this. He's the only one of us who has children. His stakes are higher than ours. We need to give him a little latitude—this is a huge opportunity for us all. There are no second chances. We've risked everything for this."

Feeling abandoned when he thought Dr. Hamid was on his side, Dr. Ogden remained silent. It felt like a wedge had been driven into their partnership, with Dr. Raj emerging as the winner.

Several weeks later, the team received the disappointing news that Accelerator was not going to fund NOVO Bio-Organic. Dr. Raj was so upset to hear the news that he disappeared without a word to his partners.

When Dr. Hamid and Dr. Ogden attempted to contact Raj, his wife covered for him, saying that he needed a leave of absence. Reluctantly the team accepted this proposal.

During Dr. Raj's absence, the division between Dr. Hamid and Dr. Ogden grew. They crumbled under the stress of not knowing where their funding would come from and if Dr. Raj would return.

ORGANIZATIONAL REPERCUSSIONS

Dr. Hamid and Dr. Ogden questioned their commitment to NOVO Bio-Organics. They were concerned they would lose their life savings and that it would take forever to rebuild, significantly affecting their careers. Their career prospects might suffer if there were a history of notable failures. All of their professional relationships risked becoming damaged. Taking a few years out of the workforce would put them far behind their peers.

Dr. Raj, Dr. Ogden, and Dr. Hamid each had the ability to bring the idea of creating immune-building drugs from bio-organic material into existence. However, the division among them damaged any potential opportunity that existed. Dr. Raj added brilliance and charisma. Until now, his positive qualities had camouflaged his flaws. Now, with the stakes higher than ever before, he could not perform under such extreme pressure.

Behavioral and Clinical Insights

It's common for leaders with borderline personality disorders to divide teams to preserve the leader's own dominance. All three scientists wanted their dream of creating a new bio-organic drug to come true. But Dr. Raj's borderline personality disorder symptoms, including his obsessive attention to his phone, excessive drinking, overestimation of his own worth, divisive tendencies, and insistence on loyalty to himself, are likely to destroy the partnership. Dr. Hamid is defending Dr. Raj out of misplaced sympathy, while Dr. Ogden is livid at what he perceives as Raj's insulting behavior that Dr. Raj and Dr. Hamid refuse to acknowledge.

The extremes of functional and irresponsible actions are common among leaders with BPD. Their talent is often so great, as in the case of Dr. Raj, that those around them think they must tolerate their actions or risk failing. They also usually care for the person, leaving them to wonder and worry if they might disappear or harm themselves with abusive behavior, including excessive drinking or even suicide. The leader with borderline personality disorder may have enablers in their lives allowing them to function. In this case, it was Dr. Raj's wife who was covering for him. Dr. Raj aches to be appreciated but has no idea how to create functional relationships with his teammates. Instead, he unintentionally keeps them all in a whirlwind of chaotic, exhausting activity.

In addition to Dr. Raj's troublesome intrapersonal and inter-personal issues with his partners, his behaviors spill out, impacting the entire organization's opportunity for success. A deeper look at Dr. Raj's history likely reveals a career-long pattern of destructive behaviors undermining achievement, much like what took place at the NOVO Bio-Organics meeting.

The behaviors of the leaders who exhibit borderline personality disorder may seem very familiar to you. Impulsive behaviors, abrupt mood swings, and excessive indulgence in destructive behaviors such as drinking are all observable traits, often excused or downplayed because these leaders are able to function at a high level of performance and, in the process, make themselves central to organizational success.

As stated earlier, the symptoms are very common because they are so treatable. Any one of these leaders can enter into treatment or be coached into taking more functional action. Treating only the symptoms, however, keeps the leader and those interacting with them in a cycle of dysfunction. The dysfunction may become more manageable over time. However, the underlying issues will remain.

Employees who work with leaders exhibiting borderline personality disorder will be inhibited from achieving their full potential. Organizations will experience operational inefficiencies, employee turnover, and unnecessary expenses. As global competition increases, individuals and organizations with such leaders will struggle to compete and advance.

Organizational Impact

THE DAMAGE INFLICTED BY TOXIC LEADERS, while often primarily felt by their direct reports, is not limited to only those in close proximity to the leader. Unfortunately, and all too commonly, the toxicity of these leaders seeps into the organization in subtle and insidious ways that result in the creation and perpetuation of a pervasive toxic culture.

When I talk about toxic leaders with diagnosable personality disorders, I often find myself blending the definition of their damaging *behaviors* with the *impact* they have on their environment. As I've previously noted, it can be very difficult to identify the source of destructive leadership. Characteristically, toxic leaders become very skilled at eluding blame, using their exceptional verbal skills and superficial charming manner to mask their corrosive behavior. What I would like to explore in this section is how observing the workplace culture can help diagnose toxicity as a first step to rooting out the source. We look for manifestations of workplace problems as a way to begin to trace them back to their origins. Remember that treating the symptoms of toxic leadership will not heal the organization. Healing can happen only when the root cause of the leader's behavior is identified and subjected to therapeutic treatment in a clinical setting and/or exposed to professional intervention that sets standards for appropriate workplace culture. This can begin with a complete diagnostic assessment, followed by coaching or leadership retraining that is recommended and coordinated by the company's HR department or more-senior-level management—or when the toxic leader is relieved of their power position or control.

There are several ways in which workplace dysfunction serves as an indicator of toxic leadership. HR partners or organizational-effectiveness consultants should always use the following key areas as critical indicators of an organization's overall health. We will look at how each one can damage an organization or business. Key areas to evaluate include:

- Employee-retention rates

- Recruitment and hiring efforts

- Promotional ladder

- Employee health

- Decision-making

- Productivity

- Low morale

- Burnout

- Trust

- Deviant, unethical behavior

LOW EMPLOYEE-RETENTION RATES

There is no one-size-fits-all number by which to calculate what is a "normal" or even an "acceptable" level of employee turnover. By "employee turnover," we mean employees voluntarily quitting their jobs without being influenced by medical conditions, early-retirement inducements, the elimination of positions, or other external factors. Certainly, there are broad industry standards—and, in some instances, even cross-industry norms—for retention rates of various positions. For example, call-center representatives, almost regardless of the industry they work in, tend to have a very high turnover rate and a low retention rate. Nonetheless, a responsible and responsive HR department should have established metrics over time for the various departments and employee positions throughout their particular company.

An investigating consultant would begin by looking at the baselines for employee turnover by department/position.

- How long have people stayed in their positions?

- How long have they remained as company employees?

- Does the company conduct exit interviews?

- What reasons for their resignation have they given in exit interviews?

Once an investigator understands the history of employee retention, they can look for trends over time. Have there been spikes or troughs in the levels of turnover? When reviewing departments or divisions separately, do some areas of the company fare better than others in employee retention? If certain departments or divisions have experienced a change recently, or if they historically underperform according to industry standards or other parts of the organization, further investigation is warranted. What variables might be contributing to the discrepancy? Have there been structural or functional changes made to this division? If so, could these have contributed to turnover? Finally, have there been changes in leadership? If so, what specifically has taken place? Could the leadership be negatively affecting retention?

New leadership often signals bigger changes within an organization. Have the goals or priorities of the division undergone significant revisions? Has the new leadership brought in talent from their previous role? Have they instituted practices intended to "clean house"? If the new leaders were transferred from within the company, what were the retention rates in their previous position?

HR professionals are well aware of the financial burden excessive employee turnover places on an organization. Although a toxic leader may be perceived as adding great value to a company, if it comes at the expense of high employee turnover, the toxic leader's "value" may be called into question.

DISAPPOINTING RECRUITMENT AND HIRING EFFORTS

HR should be able to provide background on this important area of organizational impact as well. How have their efforts at recruitment changed over time? Have they seen the number of interested applicants decline, increase, or stay flat? What are they hearing from potential candidates who decline to interview for or accept positions? If the company works with executive recruiters, what feedback have they gotten about how potential candidates perceive their company? Have there been negative comments about the company in the media or in industry publications? How is the senior-leadership team viewed by peers within their industry?

From a financial perspective, has the cost of recruitment increased? And if so, what is driving the increase in expense?

Finally, what is the acceptance rate of offers tendered? If a candidate has made it through the background check and series of interviews but declines to accept a reasonable job offer, what reasons are offered? Admittedly, it is difficult to get at the truth in these situations, but looking for a pattern may yield some insights, especially if the organization has a reputation for having a toxic culture.

In my consulting practice, I encountered a company reeling from the impact of toxic employee mismanagement by one executive. His idea was to improve the bottom line of his sales department by firing the entire senior sales team. He figured that he could rebuild a salesforce by hiring relatively inexperienced, younger, and less-expensive sales reps. It will not surprise you to learn that the mass firing of the previous sales team sent shock waves through the business community. It was viewed as a power play by the executive and cast the company in a very negative light. As the HR talent-acquisition staff attempted to fill the many sales openings, they encountered an unusual situation. Several times they offered positions to qualified candidates. The candidates waited until the last possible date to respond, and, in every case, they turned down the offers. It was as if the "word on the street" about this company was that it was a terrible place to work. The response of other salespeople in the community was to show their displeasure with the company by stalling its efforts to bring on new employees.

After restructuring the team, eliminating some positions, and assigning new titles with lower salaries to the new roles, the sales manager was unable to fill the positions needed. His department struggled, and he failed to meet his quarterly sales goals. Rather than emerging as the company hero by "saving" on labor expense, his abuse of power impacted the entire company's top-line revenues and their bottom-line profits. Even more catastrophically, the company's reputation had been severely damaged.

If the word within the industry is negative—about the leadership, the company's health and prospects, or about the work culture—the root cause may be toxic leadership. Only the most naïve, optimistic, or desperate candidates will accept an offer to join an organization with a negative reputation on any of these counts. When companies are forced to accept their second or third choices, this may have a downstream impact on turnover later, as well as poor or unacceptable performance for these less-qualified candidates. Additionally, there are bottom-line operational-cost and training-cost increases since it takes longer to get new sales reps ready to hit the streets equipped with accurate product information to meet customer needs.

BROKEN PROMOTIONAL LADDER

Healthy, growing organizations are always concerned about their "bench strength." They look to identify "HiPo" (high potential) candidates early in their careers and then put them on a path to promotion. This often involves frank conversations about the type of experience the HiPo candidate lacks, along with assignments and opportunities to fill those knowledge gaps. Mentoring, formal or informal, often plays a key role in the development of personnel. The pace of advancement cannot always be predicted, and top jobs typically don't open up all that often, especially with the trend toward delayed retirements. Still, personnel records will indicate the progress or lack of progress employees have made as they try to advance on the career ladder.

Toxic leaders characteristically will discourage the development and advancement of their direct reports, except when it serves to enhance their own prestige or position. One trait of a toxic leader with a narcissistic personality disorder is the need to always be the smartest person in the room. My experience with the head nurse of a large urban hospital offers a typical example of this damaging behavior. If other hospital administrators or even family members of the patient were present, she would often step in while one of her nurses was performing a medical procedure. She would either criticize their actions or even reprimand them publicly. Her insistence on getting involved made the nurses look and feel incompetent, when, in fact, they were providing excellent care. Her nursing staff submitted numerous formal but anonymous complaints to the hospital leadership team, stating that the head nurse's behavior undermined their ability to function at their professional best. They were trying to do their best despite the toxic culture she had created.

The strongest employees are often highly self-motivated. These true go-getters will network with their stakeholders and create positive situations for themselves. The quality of their work is often recognized by other leaders, who then handpick the high performers to join their project teams for their initiatives or programs.

Seeing their high-performing direct reports in the spotlight can put the toxic leader in an awkward position, since they do not want to provide opportunities for their direct reports to outshine them. But when approached by other managers, they have to give permission for their reports to support the work of other leaders. In this situation, often they will find ways to sabotage the direct report who is recognized as a star. The toxic leader with a passive-aggressive personality may choose to protect their own reputation by diminishing the reputation of others.

He might, for example, assign tons of other, conflicting work to the star performer to bury them under the crushing weight of too many additional obligations or responsibilities. The toxic leader may try to present these tasks as rewards for work well done, when, in fact, they are punishments meant to undermine the high performer and make them look bad. These confusing messages will often create stress, anxiety, and a feeling of being overwhelmed for the less mature go-getter employee. Employees who want to please the leader may not recognize where the tension is coming from because their mindset is designed to please the boss.

If the toxic leader is one level up from a manager overseeing a team, and that team sees its members resigning in response to the toxic culture established and perpetuated by the senior manager, the senior manager will blame the mid-level manager for the exodus of talented employees. The toxic senior leader's level of awareness is so low that he doesn't see the negative impact his behavior is having on the organization, going as deep as two levels down in the organizational structure. His mindset is limited by self-concern and self-protection, since he believes that "if the problem does not directly touch me, I can't possibly be responsible for causing it." If employees two levels down are leaving, in his mind, it can only be because his direct report, the mid-level manager, is responsible. When the impact of toxic leadership is manifested two levels down in an organization, as it is in this example, it becomes especially difficult to identify the source of the toxicity. Only the most astute HR professionals will be able to trace the source back up through the leadership ranks to identify the leader whose behavior is contaminating the larger employee base.

The toxic leader may feel they possess unique and valuable intellectual capital that must be preserved at all costs. Retaining this knowledge, they believe, protects them within the organization. They believe they are too valuable to be let go, demoted, or even disciplined. In extreme cases, I have seen organizations fall prey to this tactic. Rather than confront the toxic leader, they will implement workarounds intended to limit the damage they inflict. The senior leaders create a buffer, deciding, "I'm going to have to hire someone to manage this toxic person. I have to put somebody in between them and the team, or I'll begin to lose the team."

Organizations might also choose promotion as a way to diffuse the toxic leader's impact. The toxic leader might get promoted to senior VP to remove them from day-to-day contact, effectively isolating them on a "strategic level" where they will interact with far fewer people. Failing to deal effectively with the toxicity of such leaders carries the financial cost of creating positions that may only appear to limit their impact while placing an additional management expense on the company.

Despite limiting their direct contact with other staff, such a promotion may actually amplify the toxic leader's negative effect on the organization. A narcissistic leader, for example, will view this promotion as confirmation of their tremendous value to the organization. This perception reinforces their sense of power and authority. They will interpret this recognition as an opportunity to expand their influence across the organization. The promoted toxic leader becomes an even more dangerous force, since they feel they have earned this promotion precisely through their established patterns of toxic behavior.

Generally, a clinically diagnosable toxic leader has such a low level of self-awareness that they are unable to recognize or control their behaviors. They do not see any negative impact as being a direct result of any actions they have taken. They can have a devastating impact on employees even multiple levels beneath them in the organization without ever acknowledging that their behavior is the cause of the problem.

DECLINING EMPLOYEE HEALTH

Noting the occurrence of sick days, excused medical absences, or medical leaves can provide some useful baseline information. According to the International Organization for Standardization (ISO), the absenteeism rate is measured as follows:

$$\text{Absenteeism rate} = \frac{\text{number of absent days}}{\text{number of available work days in a given period}}$$

Chances are this data is being captured by human resources, but it may not be viewed as a symptom of toxic leadership. It's estimated that approximately 25 percent of Americans *dread* going to work. If things are so dire that employees dread showing up to work, they certainly lack the engagement and the drive to be successful in their role. Productivity plummets, lateness and absenteeism increase, and there may even be outbursts of frustration and anger. The costs to the company can be staggering, estimated to cost US employers $431 billion annually.[*]

Once again, looking for trends over time is key. However, the privacy protection surrounding health-and-wellness issues makes this an especially difficult area to investigate. Prolonged exposure to toxic leadership has been shown to cause employees high levels of depression, sadness, medical issues, stress, anger, and frustration. The result can be poor job performance, low productivity, or perhaps noticeable withdrawal from interactions with coworkers.

The costs and consequences do not stop at the workplace. I have also observed what I refer to as the "spillover effect." The employee who has been coping all day with a toxic workplace is unable to put those negative feelings aside at the end of the day. When the employee gets home and there's a bike in the driveway, or dinner isn't ready, or a teenager won't stop playing a video game—all of those frustrations from the workplace spill over into the home, causing collateral damage to relationships and families.

The types of issues that lead to "homebound spillover" not only impact the family and marital relations; they also have residual impact, boomeranging back into the workplace. In a self-perpetuating cycle, the stressed employee who sees their home life deteriorate is likely to

---

[*] *Some SHOCKING STATS About Toxic Work Cultures,* by Catherine Mattice, Feb. 3, 2021

become even less engaged and effective at work. They are now more susceptible to the pressures their toxic manager may place on them with veiled or explicit threats about their productivity or commitment to their job. The toxic leader will embrace this additional stronghold over their direct reports and use it to keep the employees kowtowing to the leader's unhealthy behaviors.

In my practice, I have seen a pattern of employees turning to the company employee-assistance program seeking treatment for depression, anxiety, burnout, or even Sunday-night panic attacks before coming to work on Monday mornings. Research indicates that employees of toxic cultures can and do experience serious medical and/or mental-health issues. Because most large organizations are self-insured, increased use of corporate medical programs will impact the company's bottom line.

CONCENTRATED DECISION-MAKING

Thriving organizations recognize that change is inevitable. To be nimble and adaptable as a business, all employees, certainly all managers, need to be capable of making decisions and be empowered to act on them. Toxic leaders are often unwilling to surrender control of even inconsequential decisions. They maintain their superiority by withholding any autonomy from direct reports. The result is organizational paralysis, with potentially profound downstream *and* upstream consequences.

I was called in to work with an organization stuck in limbo after making major changes to their organizational structure as well as building a new leadership team. For nearly twenty-four months, the entire organization had been stalled. Its employees were frustrated and uncertain about how to do their jobs on a daily basis, because the leadership was so unclear. The most senior leader was unwilling to make significant decisions. Since he held all the power within the organization, nothing was happening. The rest of the subordinate leadership team banded together to bring pressure to the senior executive. They held him accountable for the random, contradictory, and misaligned decisions he had made and for the major choices he had avoided making. Rather than accepting and acting on the responsibility he had been given, he chose to delay, avoid, and ignore complex issues. The result was crippling confusion and frustration throughout the business.

In this type of environment, employees learn to be extremely risk averse. They are afraid to do anything that might displease or anger their boss. Nothing can be undertaken that may not align with the eccentricities of the toxic leader. I have witnessed teams whose confidence and agency has been so undermined by their domineering manager that even small decisions were deferred to him. While making lunch plans one day, a member of this team suggested they all go to a nearby restaurant. "I don't know," one said, "we need to check with Mr. Smith to make sure it's okay with him." When employees are unwilling to make even such innocuous decisions independently, their risk aversion limits their ability to make meaningful contributions to the organization.

DIMINISHED PRODUCTIVITY

The people most susceptible to declining productivity are ones who were previously high performers. When they were actively engaged, these were the employees who consistently leaned into their organization. Often, they stood out for their creative solutions and novel ideas. Under toxic leadership, they have had their ideas automatically dismissed or, even worse, stolen by a senior leader who then passed the idea off as their own. It doesn't take many instances of being dismissed or not given credit before the employee will decide that their best option for self-preservation lies in practicing disengagement. Effectively, they are making a pact with themselves *not* to try to do anything but the bare minimum. No more stress, no more pressure to defend your ideas, no more embarrassment when the senior leader ridicules the ideas (and the person) or claims they alone are responsible for any success.

An often overlooked and dangerous aspect of toxic leadership is that it can occur at any level of an organization, not only at the senior-management level. Toxic leaders can sit in the middle of the organization and become destructive agents who sabotage the organization at the top and the bottom.

A large nonprofit organization selected an external candidate as their new leader. One of the new leader's direct reports had been with the organization for more than fifteen years and felt the promotion should have been given to her. She reacted to this perceived insult by being extremely agreeable in the new leader's team meetings but presenting a different face to her own direct reports. In her own team meetings, she would denigrate the leader's new initiatives and use a variety of methods to discourage her team from supporting any of the new leader's ideas.

Often, she would make passive-aggressive comments, saying things like "Let me just play devil's advocate" or "I'm not sure that will work with our clients." She did this while disguising her sabotage as "just trying to be helpful." The middle manager led her team to believe that the new leader's real agenda was to reduce the workforce, starting with their jobs. She created a toxic environment in which her direct reports did not trust the new leader.

The anxious and uncertain employees collectively decided not to lean into the new leader's vision. They aligned with their middle manager and believed it made no sense to put in any effort or energy to perform at a high level. Productivity declined dramatically for this previously well-regarded regional group.

The toxic middle manager's passive-aggressive personality caused her to wait until the low-productivity situation had come to the attention of the new leader. Then she swooped in with an "I will save the team" solution, changed her story to motivate her staff, and walked away as a hero. She reached out to the new leader's boss and casually shared that "I could get the team to work when she could not. It's more proof that I should be leading the regional team, not her."

Productivity will decline with this type of personal disengagement, at a deep cost to the organization. Even worse, toxic leadership may taint enough members of a team that they begin, consciously or unconsciously, to sabotage projects in their division. They may, publicly, assure their leader that it is a great idea but, privately, find ways to belittle, slow down, or even completely derail initiatives that have the leader's backing. Disengaged employees have decided they are not willing to endure further toxic behavior from their manager. If they do not receive recognition and support for their extra effort, then no one else will, either. Productivity declines, and, inevitably, the company fails to thrive.

LOW MORALE

People don't come to work each day intent on doing a bad job or turning in a mediocre performance. Engaged employees take pride in their ability to perform their jobs well and often derive satisfaction from the contributions they can make to a dynamic and productive team. We all want to be "winners." Possessing a feeling of autonomy and agency in one's role generally contributes to high morale.

Toxic leaders frequently come across in a self-serving way, taking the greatest care in preserving their reputation and best interests. This type of management erodes the willingness of employees to actively embrace their roles and responsibilities. If the only outcome is to build the reputation of the boss, morale suffers. Team members may find themselves attacking or undermining each other in order to gain the boss's praise. A culture of every man/woman for themselves leads to a tense, anxiety-producing environment. One team I worked with, caught up in the toxic world of a dysfunctional leader, coped by taking frequent sick days. This was so pervasive that there were very few weeks during which the entire team was present. During interviews I conducted with the team, many mentioned their running joke of asking, "Whose turn is it to be out sick today?"

Through careful, private conversations with employees such as these, it is possible to detect the reason for high levels of active disengagement within an organization. The prevalent experience of a disengaged employee is that "No one is really asking me to do anything meaningful. I just check the box. I'm putting in my time and waiting to figure out what my next move is." It is readily apparent in such situations that there is a significant organizational cost caused by low employee morale.

PERVASIVE BURNOUT

Declining productivity and low morale may develop slowly and subtly over time. Burnout can be more dramatic. Toxic leaders with diagnosable extreme personality disorders can employ a management style that fosters unhealthy competitiveness, pitting employees against each other. The targets may be unrealistic or even impossible, with the result that employees will feel pressured to produce results in ways that are unsustainable or impossible to replicate. A stressed-out employee may hit a breaking point they did not see coming. Suddenly the work pressure becomes unendurable. Employees may resign, or, less dramatically, find they are barely able to function other than to just keep showing up for work.

Too often the impossible demands of a toxic leader reveal a lack of understanding of the people and processes being challenged. A clear instance of this behavior is something I observed in a technical manufacturing site.

The science behind this product's creation required forty-eight hours of maturation to achieve the desired results. Driven by a desire to look good for improving efficiency and productivity, the toxic leader demanded that the production time be reduced to twenty-four hours. The scientists on the production team knew this was not physically possible. There was simply no way to accelerate the naturally occurring process and get the same results. Previously this team had been recognized for their technical prowess and their ability to deliver a consistently high-quality product. When they were told to cut the time in half, a scientific impossibility, as a group they felt devalued and disrespected. It appeared to the team as if their boss was accusing them of working too slowly or of being too stupid to increase production. It also revealed to them how little their boss knew about or understood the nature of their work.

Unable to comply with this irrational deadline, this once highly revered and creative team suddenly started talking among themselves about finding new positions where their expertise would be valued appropriately.

ABSENCE OF TRUST

"Flip-flopping," or a sudden reversal of position, is a tactic commonly employed by passive-aggressive or borderline personality toxic leaders. Since their top priority is self-preservation, they will adopt a different posture that puts them in a better light or even deny having previously endorsed ideas or projects that fail or fall out of favor. These self-serving reversals effectively destroy a sense of trust within a group. Employees are left to feel unsure of what they can rely on or what they can accept as true and unchanging. Consequently, their ability to make good decisions is often seriously compromised in a toxic environment. They may express this uncertainty by saying, "Because I don't trust that what is being said today will be viewed the same way tomorrow, there's no way I can make a sound decision about a way forward."

Direct reports of toxic leaders with borderline personality disorder will struggle to determine what work environment they will find every day. Borderline leaders flip-flop a great deal. One day they may exhibit a close, friendly, caring relationship. The very next day they may send a different message to colleagues: "Get away, go back to work, and just do your job." Such leaders can be very needy, one day appearing weak and the next asserting extreme levels of control.

Often the most damage is sustained by those closest to the leader. A very loyal assistant to a senior biotech executive often reported feeling abused. She referred to needing to go to an "Abused Admin Meeting" the way one would go to a support group, or even sarcastically saying she may need to check in to an "Abused Admin Shelter" after enduring an especially toxic day at work. The admin waited to see how her boss approached her each morning before committing to a mood for herself. The only happy days at work for her happened when her boss was on vacation.

In addition to tormenting their direct reports, leaders may come to rely on fostering individual competition to motivate their teams, creating a cutthroat environment. The flip-flopping leader shows they are willing to push someone under the bus if it suits them. Modeling that behavior can cause their direct reports to emulate it, keeping everyone in a defensive rather than a collaborative mode.

DEVIANT, UNETHICAL BEHAVIOR

An entire team can turn toxic behavior upon each other, imitating the behavior of the leader. Damaging behaviors such as deception by outright lying or deceiving by the omission of critical information becomes standard operating procedure in those environments. Often the toxic leaders show their reports how the very rules and policies of the company, intended to promote a positive work environment, can be re-interpreted as a means to push the line of what is acceptable. The verbally gifted leader shows how to twist the meaning and intent of company values, policy, or mission statements to justify whatever action they choose to take. They will leverage these in ways that will benefit them and even devise ways to use values, policies, and missions to dominate and browbeat the employees they have power over.

One doesn't have to look hard to find glaring examples of unethical behavior uncovered in previously highly respected corporations. When given impossible standards to meet, combined with threats to job security, employees do whatever needs to be done to keep the leadership off their backs: falsify records, misreport quality-control results, fudge the specs on a product to meet the targeted shipping date. Leaders may be issuing threats that are not even slightly veiled, telling their production lines to get that product out on time *or else*.

In my practice, I encountered a senior HR leader with a narcissistic personality who enjoyed making a sport of pitting direct reports against each other. The senior leader would dangle prime project assignments as bait, forcing the team members to stop at nothing to win overseas opportunities at beautiful company locations. Their tactics included withholding information, grandstanding during meetings, and embarrassing each other publicly by pointing out each other's flaws. During my discovery phase, I found that team members would lie to each other, lie about each other, and routinely falsify documents. Finally, one key talent broke the silence about the poisonous work culture. She threatened to leave the organization unless the group started functioning as a productive team. She was deeply concerned that the toxic behaviors encouraged by the senior leader were resulting in the sabotaging of a crucial global project. Project failure in this case could easily expose the company to legal action and to scrutiny by a federal review agency.

Fraudulent behavior usually starts at the top and then cascades all throughout the organization. You can almost consider this to be a form of sabotage. If a product fails or makes people ill or causes investors to lose a great deal of money, toxic leadership that generates deviant behavior costs an organization dearly in money and reputation, damage they may never fully recover from.

CONCLUSION

A good leader influences. A toxic leader manipulates.

With their exceptional talent for creating a powerful positive impression and their ability for self-promotion, toxic leaders very often take (and are given) credit for making significant contributions to the bottom line of their organization. Hidden behind the financial successes are the costs to the company that may be difficult to measure since the impact is mostly absorbed by employees who remain silent.

Peers who remain silent, are reluctant to report toxic behaviors, or fail to complete a 360 evaluation in an honest manner are as complicit in the promotion of toxic behaviors and cultures as the identified toxic leader. When a 360 evaluation fails to yield the truth, the toxic leader feels vindicated and even more empowered. These toxic leaders are often subsequently promoted, and their venom continues to poison the organization.

Typically, when the toxic leader finally gets exposed, the company reaction does not involve effective treatment or intervention to improve the situation. There may be some punitive action taken, but the toxic leader will look at how they got caught, build some adaptive behavior to avoid that trap, and continue on as destructively as before.

Part of the inability to intervene in a meaningful way stems from the lack of detailed information about measurable, observable incidents or behaviors. When the day finally comes when a toxic leader crosses the line, if a case has not been built over time with enough facts to justify dismissal, the company might open itself to a wrongful-firing suit. An important part of our responsibilities as HR professionals is to learn to look for and know how to record toxic behaviors that can be specifically documented. In the next chapter, I'll discuss how to employ relevant diagnostic approaches and derive clinical insights.

Diagnostic Techniques, Clinical Insights, and Consulting Practice

WHO IS THE TOXIC LEADER?

THE AMERICAN SOCIAL SCIENTIST Marci Lynn Whicker coined the term "toxic leader" in 1966, based on her extensive research and observation of executive and legislative leaders in US politics. A benchmark of toxic leadership in Whicker's definition was a person who, through abuse of power, leaves their followers and/or their organization in a worse condition as a direct result of their behavior. More recently, award-winning psychologist and professor Dr. Shonna Waters characterized toxic leadership as behaviors that are "destructive to members of a team and the overall workplace."

Toxic leadership may show up as a classic case of "I know it when I see it," especially for the unfortunate individuals whose work lives are made intolerable by toxic leaders. But "knowing it when you see it" is not nearly the same as diagnosing the underlying personality disorder. Without this crucial insight, it is not possible for HR and Occupational Development professionals to intervene and determine what corrective steps are both possible and desirable to reverse the damaging impact resulting from unrecognized, unchecked personality disorders in powerful leaders.

THE BASIS OF DIAGNOSIS

This section presents a "how-to" approach for diagnosis based on the proven techniques developed over my twenty-plus years of assessing and treating personality disorders in my practice organizations, groups, extended families, and marriages. My practice has shown that similar diagnostic techniques are as effective for business consultations as they are for private family matters. While this may seem counterintuitive, the similarities become apparent when you consider the nature of organizational behavior. Organizations are aggregations of people who have to interact and build and nurture relationships, just as family groups and married couples do. In fact, it has often been observed that, in general, we all spend more time in the company of co-workers than we do with our family members.

In both corporate and personal situations, observation of relationships reveals positive or destructive dynamics, such as use or abuse of power, trust, influence, nurturing and caring. For our purposes in this section, we will explore how a dysfunctional organization can be diagnosed like a patient, though the remedies for an organization differ from the options available to families and individuals (e.g., you can't fire your relatives!).

Without downplaying the seriousness of diagnosing toxic leadership, it's a useful analogy to think about popular TV detective shows. The plot begins with a negative event or series of events that require investigation. The looming question is "Who or what caused the event?" The detective who is called in to solve a case begins with the assumption that *everybody* in the organization, family, or enterprise, including leaders, parents, and supporters, is a suspect. HR and OD professionals have to start from the same place of neutrality and openness to determine what could be causing dysfunction within the organization. As a consultant, I look above, below, and right in the middle of the organizational chart to identify the source of the problem. No one gets a pass from my inquiry. The most effective diagnostic process starts with looking for emerging themes and then traces them to root causes, regardless of where this leads you within the levels of the organization.

The diagnostic process rests on the identification of **symptoms** indicating toxicity in an organization. How do you recognize that something is starting to happen or has been going on unchecked for some time? What are some telltale signs that trouble is brewing in your organization? HR and Occupational Development folks need to be vigilant about the *potential* for toxicity, looking for early symptoms, just as you'd notice the first indications when you're getting a cold. Early intervention as a result of careful diagnosis will help avoid major damage to the people and company.

While it is critical for HR and Occupational Development professionals to be on the lookout for symptoms, delivering an accurate diagnosis after recognizing symptoms may be beyond their specific expertise at times. As the following case demonstrates, often the best course of action in suspected cases of toxic leadership is bringing in a specially trained consultant capable of delivering an accurate diagnosis and proposing effective remediation tactics.

TOO BIG TO HANDLE ALONE

Normally Kyler was happy to run into his friend Karrie at work. The two executives often met up for coffee and candidly compared notes on their work. They found lots to laugh about and were always able to brighten each other's day. But today Kyler had just come from another stressful leadership-team meeting with Ross, senior vice president and Karrie's boss at International Talent Corporation (ITC). Kyler had hoped for a few quiet moments alone in the elevator to recover from Ross's latest unexpected and abusive "directives."

"Hey, Kyler. How's it going?" Karrie said as she stepped into the elevator. Kyler was torn. He wanted to confide in Karrie, but he was wary of complaining to her about her boss. "I'm good," he said unconvincingly. "Just tired, I guess." Karrie could tell it was more than that. "Do you have time for a coffee?" Karrie asked. "Why don't we leave the office for some fresh air and an iced coffee across the street?" It was just the invitation Kyler needed. Over coffee, he relaxed and felt comfortable enough to share his concerns. "The fact is I haven't been able to sleep well for weeks. I could handle the pressure of leading my team of seven and overseeing the operations of the dozens of people I manage, but Ross's wild mood swings are really stressing me out."

Kyler went on to describe how Ross made organizational changes to processes and structures without vetting them with the team. Ross mentioned these changes in meetings and expected instant support from his leadership team, even though this was the first time they'd heard about the new plans. If they appeared shocked or surprised or dared to question Ross, they could count on one of two things happening: getting reprimanded in their next one-on-one meeting with Ross, or worse yet, being humiliated at the next group leadership-team meeting. Ross bragged about these critical attacks, referring to his outbursts as "being put on blast."

Ross's public criticisms, using the "on blast" style, were clearly personal. He joked about team members' lifestyles or their clothes, or their regional dialect. Any direct challenge to Ross's thinking was met with the sarcastic question, "Have I done your performance review yet?"

Once Kyler started explaining his frustrations, he found it hard to stop. There were just so many examples of Ross's bad behavior. He told Karrie that he knew other managers had complained about Ross, but nothing had happened as a result. Kyler's team came to believe that Ross was "untouchable" and would soon be named executive VP of their division, with even more power over their future careers. The division, Kyler said, had been turning in outstanding results, but the fear that drove them to perform also drove people to quit to escape the intolerable workplace.

What had once been an ideal work environment for Kyler had become toxic. Under Ross's threatening and unpredictable management, the team culture of self-protection consisted of treating each other with contempt and hoarding information to be used as a weapon of self-defense at a later time. There was a lack of trust, a high level of turnover, and very little team engagement. Kyler couldn't help but wonder if it made more sense for him to leave the organization entirely rather than suffer under Ross's dysfunctional leadership style.

When Karrie heard that Kyler was seriously considering quitting, she was alarmed. "Kyler, I don't want to see you forced out of a job you love and are so good at. I know it might sound pointless or maybe even dangerous to speak out against Ross. But you have to take this to HR. We can't keep losing good people because of bad actors. There's a new HR person, who was brought on to support Ross's division. Please tell me you'll talk to her before you do anything rash like quitting." Kyler agreed to reach out. The next day, he requested a meeting with Angie, the HR business partner Karrie had recommended.

For several months, Angie, in her role as HR director, had been conducting exit interviews to try to get a handle on why so many qualified people were leaving the company. Although no one said anything directly critical of the division head in these interviews, Angie had begun to see a pattern of discontent among Ross's resigning staff. She had been attending Ross's leadership-team meetings on a regular basis and could not help but notice how quiet the team was in these sessions. Ross held the floor and did all the talking, unlike the lively, open, and participatory team meetings held by other company leaders. Angie's confidential meeting with Kyler confirmed her suspicions that something was seriously undermining the staff within this division, possibly even gaslighting by Ross.

To be effective and trusted in her role, Angie needed to maintain a neutral position, not favoring or criticizing one person or group over another. She had to be viewed by staff and management as an independent observer who could fairly resolve any conflicts. But this sensitive situation, potentially pointing to bad behavior by a successful senior executive, felt beyond her expertise. She knew her professional training did not include diagnosing personality disorders that might be the basis for abusive management practices. One misstep in evaluating the situation could damage her reputation for neutrality or even jeopardize her job security.

Angie explained the problem to her boss, who agreed with Angie's assessment. Angie's expertise was in human relations, not psychiatry or psychology. The company's best interests would be served by bringing in an objective third party. They decided to hire a consultant who had extensive experience in diagnosing management problems. They felt a qualified consultant with a background in psychiatry and/or psychology offered them the best option for uncovering the root causes of their turnover and helping to guide the HR team safely toward effective solutions.

RESOURCES FOR DIAGNOSIS: THE *DSM*

Although there are skeptics who hold to the notion that the toxic leadership behaviors exhibited by Ross are intentional and are knowingly and deliberately practiced by leaders, my work has led me to believe that *diagnosable personality disorders* are driving these destructive behaviors.

Toxic leaders do not choose to behave in a specific way. In many instances, they are wholly unaware of the consequences of their behavior. One or more personality disorders shape their actions, leading to an abuse of power that may be evident in many dysfunctional behaviors, such as blatant lying, power trips, arrogance, lack of awareness, poor impulse control, tendency toward public humiliation of direct reports, conflicts with peers, disregard for company policies and process, lack of boundaries, and the erosion of trust across the organization. The perpetrator often does not perceive the connection between cause and effect or see the possibility for alternative approaches to their management tactics.

History and Current Status of the *DSM*

Ongoing revisions since its original publication reflect the advances and evolution in modern psychiatry, psychology, and mental health. Some mental disorders have been removed from the list while others have been added. In the past, the DSM IV used a multiaxial method for diagnosing mental-health disorders. The five-axis model was broken into the following areas:

Axis I: Clinical Disorders (the primary mental disorder)
Axis II: Personality Disorders or Mental Retardation
Axis III: Medical or Physical Conditions
Axis IV: Contributing Environmental or Psychosocial Factors
Axis V: Global Assessment and Functioning (GAF), a 0-100 rating
The multiaxial system of the DSM IV separates the primary diagnosis from the personality disorder, which I believe has downstream implication for workplace impact, human-resources issues, and insurance reimbursement.

However, with the advent of the DSM V in 2013, the most current version, the American Psychiatric Association eliminated the longstanding multiaxial system for mental-health disorders. The DSM V has combined axes one to three into a single axis that accounts for mental and other medical diagnoses. There are no longer distinct categories for mental-health diagnoses, medical diagnoses, and personality disorders. Prior to the combined axes, experts argued there were no fundamental differences between Axis 1 and Axis 2 diagnoses. This change indicates that a toxic leader can have a personality disorder as a primary mental-health diagnosis.

In fairness, the DSM has had its share of criticism in areas of reliability and validity for many diagnoses. Critics fault the DSM for what they consider the use of arbitrary dividing lines between mental illness and "normality," possible cultural bias, and the medicalization of human distress.

The definitive guide, used mainly in the United States by researchers, psychiatric drug-regulation agencies, health-insurance companies, pharmaceutical companies, the legal system, and policymakers, is *The Diagnostic and Statistical Manual of Mental Disorders (DSM)*. The *DSM* is a publication of the American Psychiatric Association for use by mental-health professionals for the classification of mental disorders.

Mental-health professionals use the manual to determine and help communicate a patient's diagnosis after an evaluation. Hospitals, clinics, and insurance companies in the United States may require a *DSM* diagnosis for all patients with mental disorders.

The *DSM* is my go-to resource for diagnosis. First published in 1952, the *DSM* has undergone regular updates and revisions (a more detailed look at the changes in the *DSM* is available in the accompanying text box). As the industry standard, the *DSM* relies on empirical evidence used to standardize psychiatric diagnoses. It provides a common language and professionally accepted criteria for a wide range of mental-health disorders.

WHY USE A CONSULTANT?

Let's go back to Angie as we consider her situation and explore how to resolve the challenges she and her organization faced.

When I am brought in as a consultant, I start with a process that combines basic organizational-effectiveness/-development concepts with an overlay of solid clinical-psychology-dignostic techniques. Pursuing this blended approach is a delicate process because the workplace is not a clinical environment. In most workplaces, there are all types of protective "Watch Outs" one has to take into consideration, such as highly sensitive employment-law issues that protect and safeguard the company as well as the employees' privacy. Conducting diagnostic investigations requires careful coordination and honest communication between experienced in-house human-resource professionals and trained organizational consultants. Unlike certified coaches, who may be effective in honing leadership skills, a trained organizational consultant possesses a unique combination of skills: organizational development, an understanding of human-resource practices, and clinical expertise. The consultant's trifecta of skills enables them to achieve the desired impact within the organization without creating legal exposure for the organization or embarrassment for the leader. The consultant's ultimate goal is to significantly improve the leadership style of those in question or offer strategic options for healing the organization, transitioning the toxic leader, and preserving the positive aspects of the company culture.

When I am brought into a situation like the one Angie hired me to address, my first actions follow a standard consulting process, which allows for several variations. I add or expand the standard phases based on my experience of what the scope of work is likely to require. I recommend several authors whose books provide trustworthy descriptions of consulting approaches. These books should sit on the shelves of contemporary HR professionals. If you were only to purchase one book for handy reference, I recommend Peter Block's classic work *Flawless Consulting*. Block lays out a simple and straightforward how-to guide that brings clarity to the consulting OD process. Block's work influenced my own consulting methodology, and I have found it to be reliable, accurate, and, most importantly, highly effective.

STAGES OF INVESTIGATION AND INTERVENTION

No matter what organizational-diagnostic models you review, all will generally include some variation of the following phases, integrated within an overall OD or consulting process. The "big buckets" of the process are:

Entry → Diagnosis → Action Planning → Implementation → Termination

Depending on the consultant and the complexity of the case, each of these phases can have several subsections to assist with going deeper, executing, and following up on the plan.

After successfully completing many consulting projects regarding toxic leaders and toxic organizations, I have come to believe that the heaviest lift in the process is done in the first three phases. I place importance on these sections because they dictate "what, why, and who."

- **What** needs fixing?

- **Why** is it important to the organization and the people in the organization?

- **Who** can help, and who may be impacting the organization in a *positive or negative* way?

All successful consulting engagements must begin with the consultant establishing credibility as an expert. In your first encounter, what I refer to as the **Entry**, the client evaluates your speech and style of communication. Do you make the problem overly technical and complex, or can you speak in clear, non-jargon terms? Are you talking over their heads in an effort to seem smart by relying on too much consulting or psychological lingo? It is a fine balance of being the smartest person in the room when it comes to organizational dynamics without making your client feel dumb. The goal is to understand the issues and restate them concisely in a way that inspires confidence that:

- You have the necessary expertise

- There is hope for fixing the problem

- Solutions can be arrived at within a reasonable cost and timeline

In the entry phase, a great deal of your credibility rests on your ability to identify the problem correctly, determine the pool of stakeholders, and astutely explore all dynamics operating among those in key roles relevant to the project.

The **Diagnostic** phase is generally the second phase in the consulting cycle. This is the first fully operational phase in the process, in which you will collect empirical data that can be used to build a sound plan for intervention. The diagnostic phase examines the problem by understanding every aspect of its manifestations. Using the medical model again as a metaphor, consider the organization as the patient, while the people and processes in the organization represent the patient's organs and vital functions. What a physician would refer to as the treatment is what we in the Occupational Development world call the *solution* or *intervention* that is needed for the patient to get better.

A sound diagnostic evaluation provides the essential basis for the appropriate next steps from **Action Planning** to **Implementation**, and, when required, through **Termination**. Let's take a deeper look at what comprises each of these complex investigative stages and the resulting elements of implementation.

PHASE 1: ENTRY PHASE

a. *Exploring the Problem*

Senior leaders often believe that their company policies and culture will immediately surface what is going wrong in their organizations. My experience shows this is only wishful thinking.

The truth is that toxic leaders are good at self-protection in part because they understand and use company policies to help conceal their dysfunctional behaviors. As I mentioned previously, when I take on a new assignment, I start from the position that everyone is a suspect. They are either actively engaged in toxic behaviors, or, by their inability to recognize or condemn bad behavior, they are enabling such behaviors to persist.

I start by trying to understand as clearly as possible what my client believes the real problem is. I ask several probing questions to get at where they believe the problem is coming from. This is often not easy to do. Ironically, it may be the toxic leader themself who has invited the consultant to help solve the problem. When the toxic leader is playing the role of primary stakeholder and keeper of the consulting contract, they believe they are insulating themselves from being a primary suspect in the investigation.

I want to be clear here that I believe toxic leaders are not intentionally evil people. They will claim and genuinely hold that they want what is best for the organization (assuming it does not threaten their personal agenda). Without professional intervention, it may take years of successes and several promotions before the toxic leader is exposed as a destructive element in the organization. Toxic leaders with diagnosable personality disorders have interacted with people in this dysfunctional way their entire lives. They are really good at "passing" for positive people. They are often highly verbal, charismatic, and have a polished command of corporate speak that is highly influential. In many cases, the toxic leader realizes there is a problem in their organization and will request help from an outside consultant *to demonstrate to their leadership that they are still in control of their organization* and have only its best interests in mind. I have learned through experience how important it is in the Entry phase to always be in control of your emotions. Don't be quick to align yourself with anyone, even your client. Forming such an alliance or allegiance could cause you to miss the very source of the root cause of an organization's failings.

A useful place to begin your inquiry is to understand what is valued in the organization, and this includes processes, people, and place. Carefully crafted questions are the basis for my data collection. I want to know:

◆ Where is the power coming from? Who controls it? Why? Who has given it to them to use?

Next, I try to understand how long the problem has persisted.

◆ What was going on in the organization when the issues started? Who were the players; who was leading? What issues arose? For how long has this been going on?

Other indicators that may help me understand the dynamics:

- Who has left the organization?

- Are they available for a conversation?

- Who is new to the organization? In what roles?

I ask questions to understand if the issue is local, regional, or global.

- How widespread are the perceptions that something is amiss, or how widely are employees experiencing a problem?

- How high up the food chain is the issue known?

- How high up does the issue impact the overall business?

b. *Accepting or Rejecting the Engagement*

Based on what is known, I must decide if this situation is solvable. There's no foolproof way to determine this. Experience is the best guide. What I rely on are these considerations:

- What is the true goal of the client? Sometimes I get brought in as a "check the box" exercise so HR can say, "We tried all these things" before they proceed with a termination they were planning all along. While these situations still pay the full fee, they are frustrating, because my efforts, time, and talent could be better used someplace else.

- Does the organization honestly want to solve the issue? Is the leadership's timeline for resolution realistic for me, based on my experience and availability?

- Are all the key players available to me? Will senior leadership ensure key players are accessible on an as-needed basis for my inquiries? Will I be given full support and access to all players, including the most senior executives? (Remember, I see everyone as a suspect.)

Unless I have assurances that the intent behind the contract and engagement is genuine, realistic, and has the full support of top management, I will walk away. If you are considering hiring a consultant, you should be prepared for them to insist on these same conditions before they enter into a contract with your company.

c. *Building Project Expertise*

Depending on the nature of the problem and perhaps the type of industry, I may determine the need to bring additional expertise as a resource. As part of the transparency and honesty that should characterize the contract, I would share with the client my reason for engaging any new key players with specific industry or process knowledge to enhance how my team operates. You can't effectively challenge a company process unless you understand how the processes fit into the overall corporate picture.

d. *Designing Contracts*

Before any work is started, I build contracts with the client inside the target organization *and* with any additional expertise hired outside the target organization. In every contract, I take pains to identify what levels of commitment, how much time, and how many people I believe will be needed to assess the issues. This usually involves extensive interviews, completion of assessment tools, participation in focus groups, and potentially a variety of other activities.

Unless the obligations and expectations are clearly delineated in the contracts, clients somehow believe I will magically gather information, even though leadership teams sometimes excuse themselves from the process. Without an explicitly stated contract obligation and a mandate from the top of the house to make themselves available, senior leadership will inevitably claim they are too busy, too important, and don't have time to add my diagnostic elements to their calendar. This is often a telling sign about the level of organizational commitment and a diagnostic indication of organizational culture. The failure to commit and pledge to participate is also a deal-breaker.

PHASE 2: DIAGNOSIS

a. *Method and Discovery*

In this next most critical phase, I determine what tools are best suited for use on which group of stakeholders. Tools under consideration include:

◆ individual leadership assessments

◆ team assessments

◆ organizational-culture assessments

◆ a 360° evaluation aligned with company values

An assortment of diagnostic-assortment tools assists me in a unbiased collection of data that indicates the overall health of the organization and its leader, as well as the welfare of the individuals within it. A couple keystone tools for me is the ODDIS®, the Organizational Diagnostic and Development System and the AMP, Attachment Motivation Performance assessment. The ODDIS® and the AMP assessments, created by Bartell & Bartell, founded by Dr. Rod Bartell, one of an elite group of Registered Organizational Development Consultants in the world. He was a pioneer in employee profiling and organizational diagnostics. Bartell & Bartell continues to develop the science behind the people side of business—equipping organizations with the leadership tools and diagnostic technology to accelerate organization and leader performance.

The ODDIS® provides a benchmark assessment of organizational health. When broadly but strategically employed, it quantifies the organizational and leadership effectiveness of teams, as well as the functionality and cultural indicators of entire departments, branch offices, divisions, and organizations. Analysis of ODDIS® findings results in an organizational-needs assessment. With this information, you know where to focus the treatment, what sort of intervention (training or development efforts) will be most useful, and what leadership voids may need to be filled to restore or promote the health of the entity. The ODDIS® assesses the organization and prescribes and prioritizes interventions to optimize your intellectual capital.

Skillful use of the ODDIS® as a preventive tool provides an early-warning system, since it can identify organizational syndromes, problem areas, and hidden threats. After the damage of toxicity has been identified, ODDIS® helps pinpoint how and where toxicity may have systematically reinfected the organization. Other uses for the ODDIS® include helping to align a work group with its leader's skills, style, structure, rewards, change initiatives, and so forth. Coming soon, Bartell will be releasing a new format/version of ODDIS®, offering the ability to create your own "ODDIS package" to measure the specific organizational dimensions and dynamics that interest you the most, tailored to your preferences.

The ODDIS® offers one example of the available diagnostic tools that, when professionally applied, can illuminate which employees are ready to exit the organization, which appear to be the most affected by the toxic environment, and which may be able to assist leaders in helping right the ship. Making an accurate early diagnosis can help prevent the loss of key talent or potentially avoid even more irreversible destructive behavior against the organization or co-workers. What used to be unthinkable in the workplace is now commonplace, as we see disgruntled employees acting out in mass shootings at schools, churches, and places of employment.

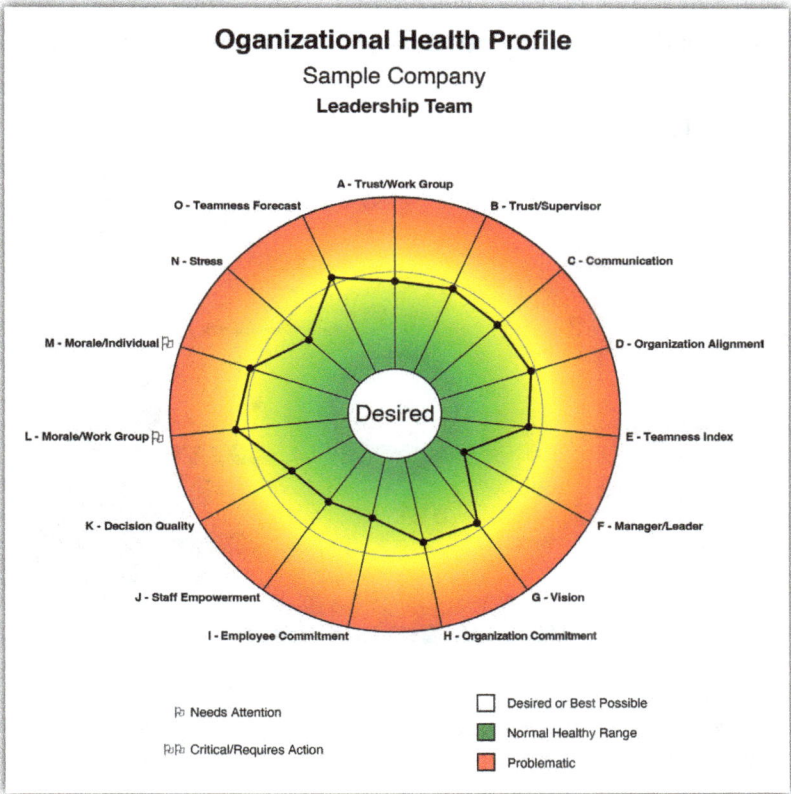

Oganizational Health Profile
Sample Company
Leadership Team

A - Trust/Work Group
O - Teamness Forecast
B - Trust/Supervisor
N - Stress
C - Communication
M - Morale/Individual
D - Organization Alignment
Desired
L - Morale/Work Group
E - Teamness Index
K - Decision Quality
F - Manager/Leader
J - Staff Empowerment
G - Vision
I - Employee Commitment
H - Organization Commitment

Needs Attention

Critical/Requires Action

Desired or Best Possible

Normal Healthy Range

Problematic

"The AMP: Attachment Motivation Performance assessment is a cloud-based solution designed to provide in-depth insight into every level of the organization. I like the AMP because it provides me with organizational information needed to create solutions for building high-performing teams and organizations. This tool allows me to analyze the team on more than 40 key stressors to determine precisely what is happening across an organization—from the department and team level, to the toxic leaders' impact, all the way down to the individual. I use the AMP to assist me in creating action-oriented strategies to help organizations retain top talent and high-potential employees, transform marginally performing teams into high-performing organizations, and retrain toxic leaders' behavior, which ultimately will strengthen overall employee attachment, motivation, and engagement." In business terms, the AMP assists in retaining talent, optimizing organizational performance, and increasing employee attachment and motivation (ROI). Below, see an abbreviated AMP report.

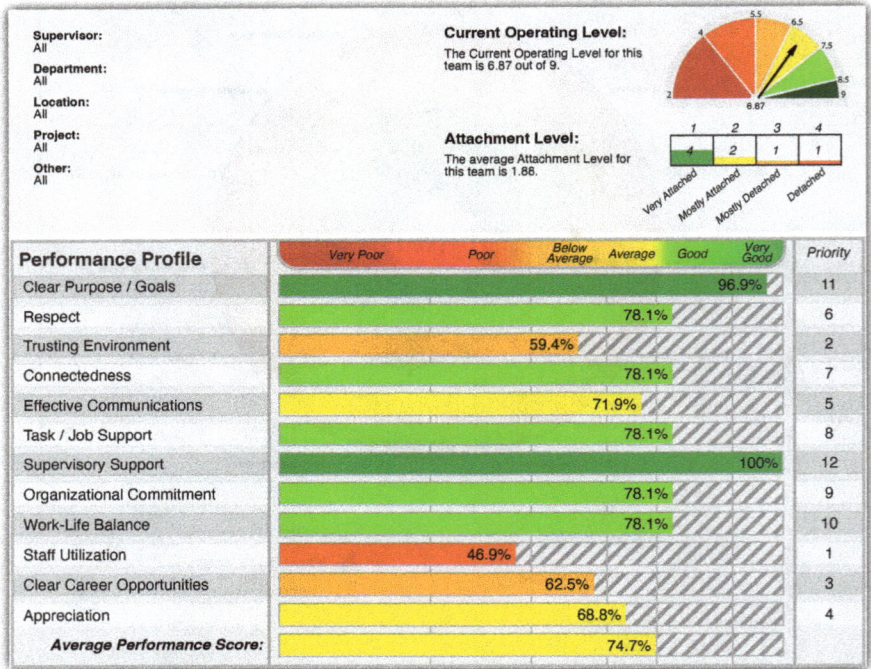

Performance Profile	Very Poor	Poor	Below Average	Average	Good	Very Good	Priority
Clear Purpose / Goals						96.9%	11
Respect					78.1%		6
Trusting Environment			59.4%				2
Connectedness					78.1%		7
Effective Communications				71.9%			5
Task / Job Support					78.1%		8
Supervisory Support						100%	12
Organizational Commitment					78.1%		9
Work-Life Balance					78.1%		10
Staff Utilization		46.9%					1
Clear Career Opportunities			62.5%				3
Appreciation			68.8%				4
Average Performance Score:				74.7%			

Another very effective tool that I use for individual assessment of a leader's style, effectiveness, and how that leader is showing up in their organization is the **Hogan**. This evaluation tool takes an in-depth look at a leader's performance capabilities, challenges, and core drivers. The Hogan tests for a combination of positive personality traits, negative personality traits (sometimes known as the "dark side" of personality),* as well as the values that leaders claim are important to them. From the information gathered by the Hogan assessment, a trained consultant

---

* *Coaching the Dark Side of Personality,* edited by Rodney Warrenfeldt, PhD, and Trish Keller, MBA

can often tease out behaviors that suggest a derailing personality style or disorders that are creating toxicity in the organization. The advantage to employing the Hogan is its science-based, objective nature. Using scientifically proven and professionally accepted tools to diagnose a well-defended toxic leader allows the consultant a safe, objective path. People and areas that might be infecting the overall organization's health can be identified without personal bias, ideally allowing for more agreement on the need for and cooperation in the creation of an effective solution.

The Hogan instrument produces three main reports.

1. Potential Report: Identifies strengths and competencies as a leader

2. Challenge Report: Addresses derailers and personality-based performance risks

3. Values Report: Lists core values and motivators for leadership

My consulting practice always uses professional and accepted diagnostic tools specifically designed to get the information I seek. It is important to note that extensive training and certification is a prerequisite to the appropriate and effective use of these tools. These are sophisticated instruments that can easily be misapplied and misinterpreted without sufficient experience and education. The decisions I have to make to begin planning my process involve:

- Determining who should be interviewed and in what order to conduct the interviews

- Deciding when focus groups are more effective than individual interviews

Using Angie and the International Talent Corporation consulting project as an example will indicate how useful these tools are. In this case, I decided it was essential to interview Ross's entire leadership team.

In addition, I conducted private interviews with every member of the peer-leadership team Ross sits on. I administered the Hogan and the more familiar Myers-Briggs assessments for Ross. For his direct reports, I used the ODDIS® to assess how they perceived their team, where they believed the team strengths and trouble areas were. Each person on the leadership team took part in a one-hour confidential interview. Then we held two small focus groups for team members to test if the individual stories changed or if, in the company of their peers, they amplified or "piled on" more accounts of toxic leadership. During the focus groups, I paid careful attention to the demeanor of the individuals within the group. I looked to see if the team was fearful of sharing and how they interacted with and responded to each other. The focus groups can sometimes bring to light a toxic leader who sits within the direct reports and may be the unofficial leader of a toxic team. Through a range of talk and tools, I was able to construct a more accurate picture of the underlying causes of stress and dysfunction.

b. *The Art and Science of the Interview*

It might be helpful here to review a chart I use that captures my interview flow, process, and sample questions.

c. *Team- and Group-Level Assessment and Interviews*

Diagnosing toxic behavior is never easy. Often the interviews themselves can be very challenging. I always start with an assessment that allows the team to share their emotions and thoughts in an objective, safe, confidential manner. Results from assessments are always reported in aggregate and *never* individually recorded, even if it is discovered that one individual is the source of toxic behaviors. This assurance fosters comfort in confidentiality and provides a safe space for all. The leadership team should be assessed and interviewed first. This action signals to the team that their concerns are being taken seriously through a process that is creditable, professional, objective, and well organized. I generally allow only seven days for the team to complete the assessment. Setting

Defining and Operationalizing the Problem

Phase 1
Define and Operationalize the Problem

TIME
No more than 1 business day post triage discussion.

PURPOSE/GOAL
Consultant needs to clarify how the client is defining the issue. Attempt to operationalize the behaviors that are being described, and always get the client's agreement.

Phase 2
"Team or Group Level" Assess and Interview Target Organization

TIME
Assessment = 7-day turnaround.
Interview = 45–60 minutes each.

PURPOSE/GOAL
Target organization should be assessed and interviewed. Allow only 7 days for the team to complete the assessment. This action signals to the team that their concerns are being taken seriously and that the process is creditable and organized.

Phase 3
Interview Only Ancillary Stakeholders

TIME
Interview = 45 minutes each.

PURPOSE/GOAL
Interviewing this audience will provide an external view of the leader and their organization.
• HR Bus. Partner
• First Level Key Stakeholders

Phase 4
Assess and Interview Leadership Team of Target Organization

TIME
Assessment =10-day turnaround.
Interview = 60 minutes

PURPOSE/GOAL
These interviews should tell you more intimate information about the organization and the leader. Based on all upstream interviews and assessments, early themes should start to emerge.

Phase 5
Interview, Assess, and Debrief Leader of Target Organization

TIME
Interview = 1–2 hours,
Assess = 90–120 minutes,
Debrief = 60–90 minutes

PURPOSE/GOAL
Note the reverse order of the assessment and interview process. Here you want to interview the leader and then use the assessment to validate the themes you heard during the interview. This phase requires debrief, which can be challenging if you have to tell the leader that their baby is ugly.

Phase 6
Only If Needed: Interview Target Organization's Peers

TIME
Interview = 30 minutes.

PURPOSE/GOAL
Consult needs to clarify how the client is defining the issue. Attempt to operationalize the behaviors that are being described, and always get the client's agreement.

a deadline signals a sense of urgency and a firm commitment to resolve the issues that are creating or contributing to a toxic culture.

It is critical that the atmosphere of confidentiality and safety carry over to the individual interviews. The interview needs to be intentionally designed and conducted to help the colleague/team member feel safe. This process cannot be rushed if it is to yield valuable insights. Often one-on-one conversations make up the majority of the overall diagnostic time.

Effective and thoughtfully posed questions are designed to lead to an understanding of whether the team is suffering from one or more toxic behaviors. Carefully scripted questions can also reveal how greatly such behaviors may be impacting the team and the rest of the organization. Some of the indicators we hope to uncover were portrayed in the case studies throughout this book as diagnosable personality disorders. The criteria for such disorders include one or more of the following indicators:

- Workplace bullying

- Counterproductive work behavior

- Job dissatisfaction

- Psychological distress

- Depression and burnout

- Frustration from inconsistent expectations

- Gaslighting

Since gaslighting has recently gained exposure, it's worthwhile to take a closer look at its characteristics. This is a form of psychological aggression and abuse similar to bullying and exclusion. Gaslighting is psychological manipulation that causes the victim to question their own version of conversations or events; at its most severe, it even leads people to question their own sanity. Building on the work of Dr. Shonna Waters, PhD, to describe signs of gaslighting in the workplace, I have refined the indicators experienced by employees to help us home in on toxic leaders who are suspected to be practitioners of gaslighting.

1. You hear persistent negative accounts of your performance.

2. You hear your leader publicly say negative things about you.

3. You hear negative, untrue gossip about yourself.

4. You find yourself questioning your perception of reality at work.

5. The leader belittles your emotions, efforts, or perceptions when confronted with these behaviors.

6. You're excluded from meetings or events relevant or required for your job, and then you get questioned about why you did not attend.

Bearing in mind all the potential information you can gather from professionally conducted interviews, it's easy to see how important they are in the diagnostic process. Let's consider this list of commonly used questions. You will note how the sample questions shown below start out as "low risk" before proceeding into more challenging and vulnerable topics.

SAMPLE INDIVIDUAL INTERVIEW QUESTIONS

1. How long you have worked at the company or in this organization?

2. Overall, do you like the company and working here?

3. What do you do here?

4. Do you enjoy your role?

    a. What part of the job do you enjoy the most and why?

    b. What part of your role do you dislike?

       i. Tell me more about that part of your role.

      ii. What makes it so challenging, and has it always been that way?

5. If I gave you a magic wand, what three things might you change about your:

    a. company?

    b. role?

    c. team?

    d. leadership?

6. Has the organization been successful in meeting its goals and objectives?

    a. If not, what barriers seem to get in the team's way?

    b. Tell me about the team's greatest success over the last year.

7. How does the team operate under pressure?

8. Do you feel as if the team has each other's back? If not, why do you think so, and do you have any examples?

9. Are there any weak links on the team? (Sometimes the team members name a specific person.)

10. Do the values of the company align with your values?

11. If not, where is there misalignment? (Please give an example.)

12. Tell me about the leader of the organization. (You might have to reinforce that this is all confidential and that the interview is a safe space.)

13. Do you trust your leadership to help the team get things done?

14. Is the leader fair with all, or are there favorites?

15. Is the leader difficult to work with? If so, in what way?

16. Does the leader have your back, or does he/she spend most of their time managing up vs. the team? "Managing up," as described in the *Harvard Business Review* Book *Managing Up and Across,* refers to the skill of effectively working with one's supervisors or managers to influence, communicate with, and support them in achieving organizational goals. However, there can be a more sinister side to managing up, in which leaders stroke their bosses' egos while treating their direct reports poorly, creating the illusion that they're influential leaders. "This toxic approach to managing isn't just unethical, it's dangerous," writes *Fortune*'s Lila MacLellan. Sep 5, 2023

17. If given a chance to move to a different department in the same role, making the same money, would you move or stay?

18. Do you feel your coworkers trust you? And do you trust them?

19. Do you feel secure in your role?

20. Do you feel positive about the team or negative?

21. On a scale from one to ten, how engaged do you think you and your co-workers are (1 being very little and 10 being extremely engaged)?

d. *Analyzing the Data*

I happen to enjoy TV detective shows, and I have even borrowed a common technique they depict. Like a detective in the squad room, I set up a white board with images of the key players, processes, and timelines. I start to piece together the story. Having the visual elements in front of me helps me identify emerging themes.

I review the results of all the assessment tools, both formal tests and interview transcripts. When consistent themes emerge, they point me where to go next in my investigation. I look to see what the team is doing well and in what areas they seem to fall short. I am constantly searching for the *why* behind the behavior.

Symptoms of dysfunction that indicate problems include:

- Lack of boundaries
- Lack of trust
  - Among the team
  - Between the team and manager
- Morale issues
  - Team
  - Individual
- "Teamness"
- Stress
- Lack of vision
- Lack of alignment
- Lack of communication
- Insecurity
- Lack of engagement
- Turnover
- Freedom to fail and how failure is treated
  - Is there learning?
  - Or blame?
- How deeply does the leader work in the organization?
- Is there micromanaging?

PHASE 3: ACTION PLANNING

a. *Defining and Operationalizing the Presenting Problem*

Getting clear about the presenting problem statement by operationalizing it allows the consultant to attach clear, observable behaviors to possibly vague descriptions of these issues by the client. This helps the consultant link his interpretation of the results of the assessments directly to the behaviors that have been described and agreed on by the client. It also helps the consultant stay neutral as he conducts the difficult conversations describing his insights and keeps him from being perceived as "personalizing" the findings. In this way, the consultant is strictly and honestly reporting what was discovered during the diagnostic phase.

Additionally, this set of steps helps with measuring impact at the end of the project. Many consultants do a great job of defining the problem but are unable to translate their findings into actions. When the consultant is able to operationalize the measurable behaviors in the presenting problem, it provides much greater clarity for anyone reading their report. What I refer to as the "operationalized problem statement" should enable someone to walk into a room and identify when the toxic behaviors are taking place and who is displaying them. This level of clarity also helps the target team hold each other accountable. In a perfect world, this knowledge and agency will go a long way toward helping the team improve their "teamness," raise their job satisfaction, promote employee retention, and contribute to an increase in the overall health of the organization.

If we return to our example of Ross's team at the International Talent Corporation, when Ross exhibits toxic behaviors, the team should be able to call them out and form a united opposition to these bad management practices.

THE LINK BETWEEN TOXIC LEADERSHIP AND PERSONALITY DISORDERS

Many of the toxic-leader behaviors can be aligned to one of the ten diagnosable personality disorders in the *DSM-5-TR*. Indicators helping to point to a diagnosis include:

◆ Poor self-awareness

◆ Arrogance

◆ "Weaponizing" organizational hierarchy to control the team and their direct reports

◆ Using favoritism to pit team members against each other.

◆ Insecurity evidenced by adamantly holding to their decisions (right or wrong)

◆ Exercising power and authority to mask lack of skills or expertise

◆ Tendency to "manage up" to more senior levels by making every action, decision, and opportunity about them. (One extreme example was a leader who set the organization's strategy so she could enjoy global travel. Although she was rarely in the office, she made sure every positive achievement by her team focused on her. If praise was not coming her way, she claimed it was a poor-performance issue by her direct report.)

The only exclusion from the otherwise comprehensive list of personality disorders in the *DSM-5-TR* is one that has received a great deal of public attention—passive-aggressive or "negativistic" personality disorder. In leaders, this disorder can show up in a variety of ways, including tendencies for:

- Procrastination

- Covert obstructionism

- Inefficiency

- Stubbornness

The *DSM-5-TR* no longer uses this phrase or label and does not count it among the ten listed specific personality disorders. It was removed because of poor evidence for the validity of the diagnosis and poor internal consistency of diagnostic criteria. Previous editions of the *DSM* described passive-aggressive personality disorder as one involving a "pervasive pattern of negativistic attitudes and passive resistance to demands for adequate performance" in a variety of contexts. Despite its exclusion from the *DSM-5-TR*, it can still be a useful way to understand what might underlie certain toxic behaviors.

To create a meaningful context for how personality disorders manifest in the population and in the workplace, the *DSM-5-TR* creates "clusters," as explained below.

1. Cluster A: People with Cluster A personality disorders exhibit behaviors others might find especially odd and inappropriate in the workplace. Cluster A individuals might exhibit unusual levels of paranoia or act with severe disinterest in people and social relationships. The following personality disorders fall into this cluster:

    - *Paranoid personality disorder.* This affects between 2.3 percent and 4.4 percent of adults in the US. Symptoms include chronic, pervasive distrust of other people; suspicion of being deceived or exploited by others, even friends, family, and partners.

    - *Schizoid personality disorder.* This is characterized by social isolation and indifference toward other people. It affects

DIAGNOSING TOXIC LEADERSHIP

slightly more men than women. People with this disorder often come across as cold or withdrawn. They rarely have close relationships with other people. They may be preoccupied with introspection and even bouts of fantasy.

- ◆ *Schizotypal personality disorder.* Odd ways of communicating and speaking, eccentric behavior, and unusual physical appearance and dress are aspects of this disorder. An individual may also hold strange beliefs and experience great difficulty forming any relationships.

2. Cluster B: Dramatic and erratic behavior suggests that individuals are suffering from one or more of this group of personality disorders. People in this cluster tend to either experience and act on very intense emotions or engage in extremely impulsive, dramatic, promiscuous, or even illegal and unethical behaviors.

- ◆ *Antisocial personality disorder.* Often this disorder surfaces in childhood, unlike most other personality disorders, which do not manifest until adolescence or young adulthood. Early symptoms include a total disregard for rules and social norms, as if the person were exempt from all commonly accepted modes of conduct. Quite often such individuals also display a complete lack of remorse for any injuries to or suffering by other people.

- ◆ *Borderline personality disorder.* The key feature of this disorder is instability. This shows up as constant and unpredictable changes in interpersonal relationships, emotions, and self-image. As a consequence, the individual engages in what seem to be inconsistent and impulsive behaviors.

- ◆ *Histrionic personality disorder.* A person with this disorder is the one co-workers refer to as the "drama queen." They are given to excessive emotionality and attention-seeking that can prompt them to adopt socially inappropriate behavior to make sure the spotlight is on them at all times.

◆ *Narcissistic personality disorder.* This is generally associated with self-centeredness. It can show up as an exaggerated self-image and lack of interest in and empathy for others. Very often narcissistic personality disorder has at its basis an underlying fragility in the sense of self.

3. Cluster C: A tendency to experience anxiety is the common thread of this cluster.

◆ *Avoidant personality disorder.* Feelings of inadequacy and dread of criticism lead to patterns of social inhibition and avoidance of others.

◆ *Dependent personality disorder.* This is the opposite behavior, in which fear of being alone causes those with the disorder to try to tie other people to them, often in caregiving roles.

◆ *Obsessive-compulsive personality disorder.* Individuals with this condition are preoccupied with orderliness, perfection, and control of all things, including relationships. While obsessive-compulsive personality disorder (OCPD) and obsessive-compulsive disorder (OCD) have similar names, the clinical manifestations of these disorders are quite different.

Unlike OCD, obsessive-compulsive personality disorder is *not* characterized by intrusive thoughts, images, urges, or repetitive behaviors. OCPD involves an enduring and pervasive pattern of excessive perfectionism and rigid control. For example, a leader who requires things be *done right* in highly detailed and specific ways might have an OCPD. Unfortunately, often this controlling behavior gets rewarded on the job! It can reach a level of toxicity when the leader uses their position to bully and make unreasonable demands of direct reports under the guise of "getting it right."

For the purposes of this book, I will specifically focus on two personality disorders from Cluster B in the *DSM-5-TR*, borderline and narcissistic, since these are very common elements of toxic leadership. And although passive-aggressive behavior is not in the *DSM-5-TR*, I will include this disorder in my discussion as well. My consulting experience indicates there is enough diagnosable evidence of passive-aggressive behaviors in some toxic leaders to warrant its inclusion.

Since I believe in the link between toxic-leader behavior and personality disorders, I typically add clinical questions designed to get at the root cause of behaviors when I interview the organization's leaders. Leadership questions can be most revealing when they focus on how the leader *believes* they show up to their team or organization. It takes a trained consultant with extensive clinician expertise to detect in the interviewee's responses indications that some of the diagnosable criteria may be present. Expertise and experience are key. Very often the leaders being interviewed are extremely bright people who believe they can "out-think" the questions and skew the assessment in their favor. Effective use of interviewing is essential since, when done professionally, the process provides information that helps shape the possibilities for creating an appropriate intervention and/or solution.

The following list suggests the type and range of questions I commonly employ.

Questions:

1. Tell me about your background here at the company.

2. How long have you been in a leadership role?

3. How do you believe you show up for the team?

4. Have you ever completed an engagement survey or a 360 survey?

5. Would the team say you are a patient leader or an impulsive leader?

6. Do you feel overwhelmed by this role?

7. How do you manage your anger?

8. Complete this sentence . . . "If it wasn't for me, this team would . . . (act how or do what)"

9. Are there any of your direct reports who appear to struggle to align with your leadership style? If so, how do you respond to this?

10. On days when you feel the most under pressure, how do you generally show this to the team and your peers?

My practice has helped me develop a set of standards and protocols for these interviews. Where possible, I try to keep all my questions open-ended, avoiding the option for "Yes" or "No" answers. As with all effective interviewing, it is critical that the consultant do far more listening than talking. Encouraging the leader to give full and detailed responses will yield more insights than brief, knee-jerk replies. Interviews should be conducted in a quiet and private space, free from distractions like cell phones and computer screens. I find it useful to set an expectation for the time it will take and to have the interviewee set aside an agreed-upon amount of time for our conversation.

With the interviewee's permission, I may record the exchange, though I will also take brief notes while we are talking. I want to establish a comfortable and trusting tone, but I avoid reacting to or registering emotion at any of the interviewee's remarks. At most I will exhibit curiosity, often asking the leader to tell me more about their statement. I always end by thanking the individual for their time and, when appropriate, letting them know of any next steps.

PHASE 4: IMPLEMENTATION

Before I walk through this complex next stage of the consulting process, it's worth considering the layers of ambiguity that surround activities that make up *both* the diagnosis *and* the recommendations. Organizations, because they are made up of human beings, are extraordinarily complicated. Over time, organizations develop what we refer to as "company cultures" and even "personalities." Individuals within the organization may be acutely aware of the culture, and they may be inclined to protect it or avoid disrupting it. The same can be said of its leaders.

In the short cases we've looked at earlier in this book, leaders are shown to be capable of profoundly affecting those around them and the organization as a whole. Good leaders do just that in positive ways. They are not afraid to coach, to give credit for innovation, and to recognize and reward hard work. They communicate a clear mission and vision and give their teams a solid sense of belonging. Standards are clear, consistent, and equitable. Under these conditions, employees feel empowered to work to their fullest capacity without fear of failure.

Poor leadership too often results from entrusting unsuitable, insufficiently skilled individuals with power and authority, especially when they also suffer from a personality disorder. Most people are simply not cut out to be leaders. Many people recognize this about themselves but, when offered more money and prestige, are unable to turn it down.

Depending on the overall culture of the organization, such a refusal of promotion can be viewed as career suicide. But stepping into a leadership role for which you are unqualified may exacerbate a thirst for power and trigger the fear of losing that power, especially once you have tasted it. Sometimes it is the pressure of being expected to lead that causes a diagnosable personality disorder to surface.

Most psychometric tools that I use for diagnosing a toxic leader or organization provide a profile for behavior under *both* normal conditions *and* under pressure. When an individual with an underlying personality disorder and a desire for power within a power-driven organization undergoes stress, the result is a scary trifecta of ingredients—namely power/control, toxic organizational culture, and diagnosable personality disorders—likely to cause an explosion. In these volatile situations, it is more difficult to pinpoint if the leader is toxic or if the leader stepped into a toxic organization.

There are several variables that will cause this quick reaction. The response may be to expose a toxic leader or a toxic organization, or it may be defensive pushback by staff against the threat of change. Determining factors to consider are:

a. *Mean age of the team*

Older, more-seasoned employees are often less comfortable with change and may reject the new leader's style as threatening.

b. *Mean years of service working together*

Teams with longevity working together are very protective of their processes. Anything that might disrupt their familiar work environment can be labeled as poor leadership.

c. *Misinterpretation of the leader's style*

All leaders have an established style for how to engage and motivate the team. If that style is dramatically different from what the team was accustomed to, they may label it as "bad" leadership, if, for example, the team had a previous leader who was completely hands-off while the next leader was more fully engaged.

d. *Toxic direction from upper-level management*

This is often a factor when senior leadership is being forced to drive change for budgetary reasons or sometimes for change itself. The challenge to move the organization often lands on the shoulders of middle managers. Studies such as "Piggy in the Middle: The Challenges and Value of Middle Management"[†] and "Why Being a Middle Manager Is So Exhausting"[‡] have shown that leading from the middle of the organization presents significant problems. This can become a case of "shooting the messenger."

Toxic leadership can be the byproduct of many actions. However, taking a close look at the classic contributing factors—power/control, toxic organizational culture, and diagnosable personality disorders—is where any investigation of root causes should begin.

SHARING THE FINDINGS

It might seem counterintuitive to describe my implementation process as one of full disclosure and transparency. After thoughtfully and objectively weighing the findings from the multiple assessment tools, an accurate diagnosis sets the course for what happens next. Often problems exist on both the clinical, individual level and at the organization or structural level. To bring about lasting improvement, both layers have to be addressed, with equal commitment by the individual and the senior leaders to take action.

When the root cause emanates from the organization, candor is the first step. I always start my intervention by sharing the outcome from all the diagnostic processes. It's important for credibility and trust that all the cards are laid on the table, visible to all participants. Everyone, including the leader under scrutiny, needs to be aware of what I am seeing and hearing. They need to see not just the dynamics at play but also (and most importantly) how everything is impacting the performance of the team and causing ripple effects beyond the team.

If the issues surrounding the leader are especially sensitive or severe, I will meet with that leader privately first, or perhaps in the presence of

† LinkedIn article, Nov 7, 2022, by Verity C.
‡ *Harvard Business Review*, March 22, 2017, by Eric M. Anicich and Jacob B. Hirsh

my client contact (e.g., the HR executive). This initial meeting shows respect for the leader as an individual but also enables me (and the client) to determine how committed the leader is to resolving the situation.

In the debrief, I speak very directly about what the data from the psychometric tools and the interviews have told me. I relate how others believe the leader shows up to the team and to their peers and colleagues. Part of my message is a clear statement that how they are perceived will find its way to senior management. When senior leaders become aware of toxic traits, it could permanently derail career advancement. When my diagnosis involves clinical personality disorders, it adds to the sensitivity of the disclosure. This information *must* be shared with the client contact as well as with the individual. It is important to carefully word this information to avoid violating HIPAA (Health Insurance Portability and Accountability Act) privacy regulations.

The way in which leaders under scrutiny respond to the information I disclose gives a clear picture of their openness, honesty to admit the need for change, and their sincerity about doing the necessary work. If the toxic leader tries to downplay the findings or dodge the consequences by saying things like "we need to table this for now, because we're too busy to get distracted," it's a telling sign of a deep-rooted problem that will probably prove to be unresolvable. Organizations deal with this conclusion in a variety of ways. An attitude like this may result in termination. Sometimes the leader is promoted to a more powerful position, or the organization may hire someone to serve as a buffer to that leader. It is up to the senior management to make the judgment call, taking into consideration the larger repercussions to the overall organization.

After concluding a full debrief with the leader individually, I meet with the entire team. This situation has its own pitfalls. It is essential to share the results of the investigation while protecting the privacy and confidentiality of all participants. I walk a thin line between not exposing the team as the villain and not sharing confidential medical information that could compromise the leader. I present all the data in a composite format, being mindful to speak in terms of *behaviors* and the impact those behaviors have on the overall performance and output of the team.

It is often desirable to hold these full-team debriefs at an offsite workshop environment. Moving them away from the office fosters a greater sense of privacy and safety for the team. An offsite session is also far less likely to be plagued by interruptions and distractions.

There are a number of custom interventions I have found to be very valuable for team debriefs. A fun icebreaker activity helps establish the tone for the meeting. Next is a custom-designed interactive game, activity, or project, etc. This could take from forty-five to ninety minutes, followed by discussion about the exercise. These activities are designed to encourage the team to work together in a "business as usual" (BAU) mode, which will generally expose several toxic issues. The leader is required to participate in the group activity, which is how many of the toxic behaviors will generally surface. These scenarios are intended to shine a light on toxic behaviors, illuminating where they could be coming from. The group activities take place before the debrief of the diagnostic-tool data. I use these results of the activity as an example during the diagnostic debrief to further drive the learning points and insights from the investigative-evaluation process.

As a rule of thumb, I generally design these interventions and debrief sessions to take a minimum of one full day; in most cases, they run for one and a half to two full days. Toxic team issues that are triggered by leadership can make for extremely emotional interventions. Allowing sufficient time for the team to take part is critical. The debrief process requires time for deep communication, reflection, and acceptance before the team can work through their experiences with toxic behaviors and begin to find a way forward.

Using a process called **Team Charter,** a valuable product of this group work can be created through a solid and well-facilitated activity encouraging the team to describe their preferred ways of working. The Team Charter intervention works like a "mulligan" in golf. It gives the team a "do-over" or team reset, allowing them to design a fresh start for their interactions. This activity is powerful because it allows team members to recognize and call out even more dysfunction in their interactions and processes. In this exercise, the team creates a structure and safe method to address the toxic behaviors holding them back. This methodology allows the team to separate what issues come from within the team and what are reactions to external "uber" toxic cultural-organizational issues from outside the team. When teams do the work of writing their own charter, a sense of newness and promise often gives them hope. Being able to describe their ideal ways of working inspires them to try to move ahead in a more positive way.

Elements of the Team Charter to be decided upon include:

- Re-establishing the team purpose

- Setting goals and objectives

- Evaluating daily work processes

- Defining team roles and responsibilities

- Recognizing interdependencies

- Establishing metrics

- Describing team culture

- Formalizing decision-making

- Creating methods for shared work and information

- Establishing effective methods of communication

- Committing to team accountability

TERMINATION: CLOSING OUT A CONSULTING PROJECT

Responsible, worthwhile consulting work should have a definite starting point and an equally clear and agreed-upon end point. Consultants who try to engineer a long-term "never-ending" project may not have the organization's best interests at heart. Many professional consultants like me have had to work hard to overcome this classic stereotype of the consultant who prolongs the work to prolong their compensation. Consulting should be a professional intervention designed to uncover the root cause of a problem, propose a solution, and assist with the development of a practical and pragmatic implementation plan over a specified time frame.

The end point and its deliverables (scope of work) should be carefully described at the start of the contract. During the contract term, the consultant should be working toward this specific set of goals and achievements in a timely manner. However, it is the client's decision to consider the work complete or to extend the contract after a discussion and evaluation of the intended results has been conducted. If the intended results have not been achieved and more intervention is required, then the consulting contract can be extended until the desired outcomes have been reached. It is not uncommon for the initial exploration and intervention to reveal other areas that require further professional attention. The client may choose to revise the contract, extending it to other areas of the organization and redefining the deliverables and outcomes.

All trustworthy consultants should be willing to honestly evaluate the project and determine the extent of success attained. If the intervention has been a moderate to high-level failure, the consultant may advise terminating the consulting contract. Or they may suggest re-evaluating how the client might achieve the desired results with or without their continuing consulting services.

When done well, the launch and conclusion of the consultant's work should be so smooth that the organization doesn't undergo any disruption. Ideally the consultant's entry is unobtrusive, and their work brings positive benefits to the organization by enabling it to sustain the new desirable behaviors without creating turmoil.

To achieve ongoing success after the conclusion of a project, a key aspect of the exit process is the identification of individuals in the organization who will accept responsibility for managing the new behaviors and holding the organization accountable for the new language, processes, and actions. This person (or team of people) should work alongside the consultant throughout the contract to ensure a firm understanding of how to support the changes undertaken and institutionalize them into the organization.

Managing the transition from the consulting project to the internal "compliance" person goes a long way toward making changes endure. The consultant wants the key stakeholders to see that the contracted tasks have been completed and that someone (or a team) is in place with the knowledge and authority to make sure the impact of the project continues. No consultant ever wants the stakeholder to ask after the fact, "Now, what did we pay all that money to the consultant for?"

I recommend the following procedure as a way of successfully closing out a consulting project: Hold a formal closure meeting with all stakeholders. The attendees should include anyone who touched the work or has control over any impacted organizational policies.

To be sure that there is full agreement over the work that has been done, I generally partner with the key stakeholders to present the original trouble statement, the identified departments, the intervention, and timeline for completion. I lay out findings succinctly and clearly. It's always helpful to show results before and after impact by way of demonstrating what got better, what stayed the same, and any negative setbacks. I then lay out a plan for continuous improvement within the organization. This entails a clear set of recommendations for how to move forward and who will be responsible for managing the new culture. This meeting provides closure for the consultant while empowering those who will now step up and continue to do the work of enhancing and preserving the improved culture.

The final step in this process is completing what I refer to as a "sustainability plan." Making a commitment for a follow-up in the near future allows the consultant an opportunity to come back and reconnect with the key stakeholders, the team, and the organization to ensure everything is still working as planned. I suggest a follow-up engagement take place three to six months after the conclusion of the consulting contract. As part of the post-evaluation and sustainability plan, I like to conduct a few short interviews with some of the original participants. Following these conversations, I generally send a letter to the key stakeholders, letting them know the intervention is still working. If problems have arisen, I provide recommendations for any adjustments to keep things on track. It's rare that I recommend returning to do more of the same intervention. I offer this "sustainability plan" at no cost to the organization. I find it brings real value for the client and builds goodwill with the key stakeholders for future work and referrals.

The Future
of Work

THERE IS A SAYING THAT GOES: "People don't leave jobs—they leave bad leaders." Conversations with employees, colleagues, direct reports, key workers, and countless others over the years suggest that the corporate work culture has changed dramatically, and not for the better. Where once many employees felt safe and believed that their work environment offered them a great place to work, learn, and grow, there is increasingly a belief that this type of employee-centric culture is a thing of the past. The main theme shaping current company cultures is making more money for shareholders by any means necessary, even at the cost or loss of talented, loyal, hard-working employees.

Upper-level leaders are under relentless pressure to deliver aggressive promises to achieve double-digit growth for shareholders. This pressure fosters a toxic environment that trickles down throughout the organization, beginning at senior levels and then infecting mid-level and frontline leaders, who pass the pressure along to the workforce they supervise. Stressed leaders often engage employees with aggressive, mean-spirited, and disrespectful bullying behaviors as the most-effective method to meet unreasonable, unrealistic deadlines and product requests. Pressing for accelerated results within processes that are already maxed out, or demanding unreasonable gains in productivity never ends well. No matter the skill or intention behind the procedure, it really does take three minutes to make a three-minute egg. An inflexible edict to go faster than is possible jeopardizes employee safety and product quality. The consequences are not lost on the labor force.

Employees are reporting what they perceive as a shift in the company's role, moving away from an ally helping its workers build a secure life for themselves and their families, to an adversarial relationship where the mantra is "watch your back." Even upper-level workers feel the uncertainty expressed in the advice to "keep your head on a swivel" since dramatic, unexpected changes might happen at any time. Mid-level and senior managers report spending more time managing the fallout from toxic culture than focusing on more substantive work. And in a related development, we are witnessing more support for unionization, especially among younger employees in companies such as Starbucks and Amazon who perceive unions as a form of protection.

In the years leading up to the COVID-19 pandemic, employees were starting to realize that the hiring process was a two-way street. Young talent entering the workforce began to be more selective about what they expected from a work culture before they were willing to sign on with a company. In 2018, the workplace consultancy Gallup polled Gen Z and Millennials to learn what they most valued in an employer. The answers of the two groups were surprisingly similar. In fact, these themes have been apparent only over the past year, as post-pandemic worker shortages limit many companies' ability to grow. The pandemic has brought many of these "nice-to-have" items to the forefront, turning them into deal-breakers for Millennials and Gen Z workers if companies don't have these traits or have a poor reputation for delivering on these needs. Before looking at the key demands of these cohorts, it's worth reviewing a timeline of the demographics of the American workforce.*

Listed below in order of importance are what Millennials and Gen Z named in the Gallup survey as the key elements that make up an attractive company culture.

1. **Above all, Gen Z and Millennials want an employer who truly cares about their well-being.**

---

* Chart created by the author.

Generations by Birth Time Period

	Silent Generation	1928●1945
	Baby Boomers	1946●1964
	Generation X	1965●1980
	Millennials/ Generation Y	1981●1996
	Zoomers/ Generation Z	1997●2012
	Generation Alpha	2010●2025

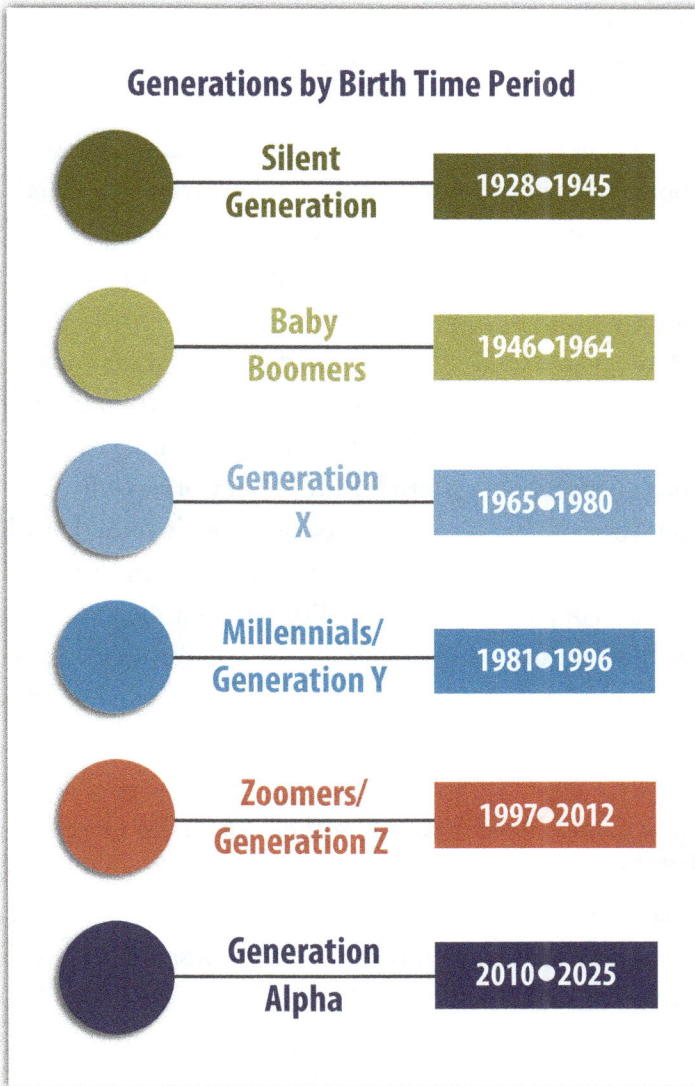

The year 2020 brought employee well-being into sharp focus. Many employers quickly learned that, if the people in their organizations aren't healthy—both physically and emotionally—the organization isn't healthy, either. While COVID-19 underscored this critical fact, a company's focus on employee well-being has long been a decisive factor in attracting workers and shaping their feelings about their employer. In fact, a company's commitment to employee well-being was in the top-three issues for *every* generational cohort before the pandemic. Most organizations have wellness programs of some sort that generally focus on physical health, but for employees, physical wellness isn't enough. For example, young employees may be physically healthy but suffering from social isolation or other mental or emotional factors that hinder their productivity. Stress and anxiety from social isolation can especially impact minority employees whose work requires them to live in areas that are underrepresented by their cultural background. Entry-level workers with insufficient earning power may be experiencing acute financial hardship that affects their daily performance. Going beyond the traditional markers of physical health, Gallup has identified five elements of well-being: **career, social, financial, community, and physical.** Each element influences the others, and thriving in all of them is necessary for a healthy work-life balance.

2. **Gen Z and Millennials want their leaders to be ethical.**
    The year 2020 was record-breaking for SEC fines and penalties resulting from corporations violating codes of conduct and regulations. The media has also covered high-profile scandals of young entrepreneurs fabricating results, scamming investors, and enriching themselves at company expense. Young generations have grown up watching breaking news of unethical behavior as one success story after another is revealed to be the work of con artists. Even highly respected banking, automobile, and pharmaceutical corporations have been found guilty of malfeasance and grave ethical failings.

    Without question, scandals are toxic to the overall health and success of any organization. The fallout for unethical behavior now goes well beyond being a matter of compliance shortcomings or public-relations issues. Employees want their leaders to do more than the legal minimum required, not tout empty platitudes in their company mission and vision statements. Younger employees expect their employers to take bold action by acknowledging and correcting existing moral blind spots in areas like social justice, the environment, gender identity, abortion, gun violence, and personal rights. In addition, the new workforce wants to know that the work they are doing on behalf of their employer has a net positive impact on human beings and the natural world. Companies with global footprints have even more issues impacting their workforce. Ethical leadership must address the external social issues that their workforce values. This is more than a simple matter of productivity. Valuable employees want a relationship with their employer that is based on trust, and trust begins when every worker believes they are being treated fairly and are heard by their leadership. I'll return to the issue of trust a bit later when I discuss how to build a nontoxic leadership and company culture that looks to the future.

3. **Millennials want open, transparent leaders.**

The Millennial generation introduced the trend toward supporting leaders who are open and transparent in their communication and management style. Notably, COVID-19 compelled many corporate leaders to behave with greater transparency. The sudden and severe disruptions caused by the pandemic required leaders to engage respectfully in straight talk with employees as one way to allay their uncertainties and anxiety for their own well-being and that of their families. Virtually every type of business had to restructure and redefine their ways of working in order to enable the business to continue to operate. Many of the long-established rules and beliefs about work flew out the window, replaced out of necessity by innovations and new ways of accomplishing all sorts of tasks.

Employee engagement in the US rose over the past year.[†]

Chief human resource officers (CHROs) from the world's largest corporations are quick to point out the increased level of communication between all levels of management and line workers. Though much of this communication was virtual, CHROs feel it was effective in enabling their companies to perform. As the country emerged from the pandemic, many employees have shared that they felt they worked harder and longer while working from home. Companies can't dispute the fact that work continued at every level of the organization while employees were not face-to-face in the office. Given that, the big question employees are asking organizations now is why they are requiring employees to spend two to four hours per day commuting to work three to four days each week in the office. Leaders who are unable to address this unpopular decision with an open and transparent explanation are at risk of losing talented employees, who will move on to another company offering a better work-life balance, with more control over their work environment.

4. **Gen Z and younger Millennials expect a diverse and inclusive workplace.**

These demographic groups grew up in a far more diverse American society than previous generations. They demand respect, equity, and inclusion for who they are and how they identify—and they are voting with their consumer dollars and employment choices. Diversity, equity, and inclusion (DEI) is not a "nice to have" concept for this generation. It is an imperative, at the core of their identities.

While US employee engagement showed a calendar-year surge in 2020,[‡] it took an historic drop in the summer during the George Floyd protests. Many corporate leaders took notice. DEI is now a top priority for business leaders across the country—as

---

[†] "State of Engagement 2023: Shifting from Survival to Long-Term Success," Ross Brooks, May 1, 2023

[‡] https://www.gallup.com/workplace/391922/employee-engagement-slump-continues.aspx

it has been for younger workers for some time. One way to think of DEI in the workplace is *individualized respect.* Young people want to be appreciated for their unique contributions, and they want to feel valued. As with ethics, DEI is not just a question of corporate policy. It affects how employees accomplish their daily work. Disrespect breeds distrust, which destroys collaboration and honest communication. Respect and recognition matter from every direction—peers, managers, policies, systems, and leaders. Much like the discussion of ethics, a "Do no harm" approach to DEI is not enough to create the sort of inclusive culture younger workers value.

5. **Lack of "learning and leadership-development" programs can be a deal-breaker.**

    Younger generations expect to be coached, mentored, and developed as a way to advance in their workplace. They expect that, from the start of their employment, they are being groomed for the next level or opportunity. Organizations that lack robust learning and development programs are putting themselves at a disadvantage for recruiting and retaining top talent. Gallup analytics show that Millennials are more likely than the previous generation to say that "development opportunities" and the "quality of the manager" are extremely important in a new job. Young employees want a manager who cares about them as people and who is actively engaged in their career growth. Younger employees are more likely to call out cultures and leaders that create toxic environments. Leaders and organizations with poor reputations will not be able to attract the talent they need for future growth and viability.

To create a non-toxic and highly desirable environment, organizations have to look at the total ecology of their workplace. As this graphic illustrates, only when all of these pieces are seamlessly connected will an organization be able to secure and protect its most precious resource—its people.[§]

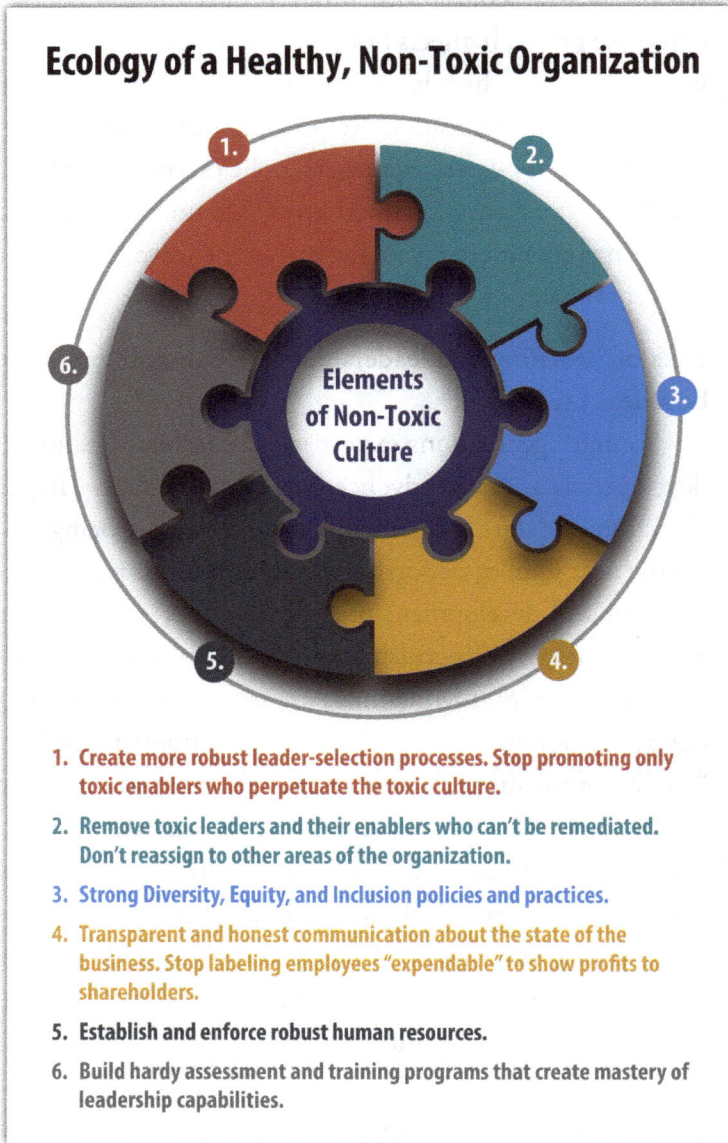

Ecology of a Healthy, Non-Toxic Organization

Elements of Non-Toxic Culture

1. Create more robust leader-selection processes. Stop promoting only toxic enablers who perpetuate the toxic culture.

2. Remove toxic leaders and their enablers who can't be remediated. Don't reassign to other areas of the organization.

3. Strong Diversity, Equity, and Inclusion policies and practices.

4. Transparent and honest communication about the state of the business. Stop labeling employees "expendable" to show profits to shareholders.

5. Establish and enforce robust human resources.

6. Build hardy assessment and training programs that create mastery of leadership capabilities.

[§] Graphic created by the author.

Shown below is a list of corporations that have met the algorithm standard created by Workforce Logiq, a provider of artificial-intelligence technology. This assessment sought to rank workplaces in which workers were the least likely to resign or want to leave the company. The perceived quality of executive leadership emerged as one of the main indicators for employee retention.

---

1. **DuPont**
   Headquarters: Wilmington, Delaware
   Share of employees likely to quit: 20 percent.
   Number of employees: 98,000
   Strongest retention factor: Company resilience

---

2. **Honeywell**
   Headquarters: Charlotte, North Carolina
   Share of employees likely to quit: 23 percent
   Number of employees: 114,000
   Strongest retention factor: Company resilience, **strong leadership**

---

3. **Lockheed Martin**
   Headquarters: Bethesda, Maryland
   Share of employees likely to quit: 25 percent
   Number of employees: 105,000
   Strongest retention factor: Tie among company resilience, career growth, positive environment, business stability, **strong leadership**

---

4. **Delta**
   Headquarters: Atlanta, Georgia
   Share of employees likely to quit: 15 percent
   Number of employees: 88,700
   Strongest retention factor: **Strong leadership**

5. **Merck**
   Headquarters: Kenilworth, New Jersey
   Share of employees likely to quit: 28 percent
   Number of employees: 69,000
   Strongest retention factor: Company resilience, **strong leadership**

6. **Amazon**
   Headquarters: Seattle, Washington
   Share of employees likely to quit: 42 percent
   Number of employees: 647,500
   Strongest retention factor: **Strong leadership**

7. **Microsoft**
   Headquarters: Redmond, Washington
   Share of employees likely to quit: 43 percent
   Number of employees: 131,000
   Strongest retention factor: **Strong leadership**

8. **Intel**
   Headquarters: Santa Clara, California
   Share of employees likely to quit: 25 percent
   Number of employees: 107,400
   Strongest retention factor: Company resilience, positive environ-
   ment, **strong leadership**

9. **Best Buy**
   Headquarters: Richfield, Minnesota
   Share of employees likely to quit: 21 percent
   Number of employees: 125,000
   Strongest retention factor: **Strong leadership**

10. **American Express**
    Headquarters: New York, New York
    Share of employees likely to quit: 30 percent
    Number of employees: 59,000
    Strongest retention factor: Positive environment, **strong leadership**

11. **Cisco**
    Headquarters: San Jose, California
    Share of employees likely to quit: 34 percent
    Number of employees: 74,200
    Strongest retention factor: **Strong leadership**

12. **The Coca-Cola Company**
    Headquarters: Atlanta, Georgia
    Share of employees likely to quit: 20 percent
    Number of employees: 62,600
    Strongest retention factor: Company resilience, **strong leadership**

MOVING TOWARD A HEALTHY WORKPLACE

Armed with a deeper, up-to-date understanding of what the current and future workforce expects from an employer, wise organizational leadership can create an enduring competitive advantage for their companies by settling for nothing less than a robustly healthy workplace. One fundamental change requirement is moving away from behaviors that treat workers as expendable. Over the past few decades, American corporations have been through "downsizing," "right-sizing," and "adapting to a new scale"—these are just some of the euphemisms applied to layoffs and workforce reductions. What may have begun as a periodic response to market conditions in many instances became a habitual practice, as companies realized that pushing productivity gains through labor reduction boosted profits.

In extreme cases, companies have gone way past "cutting out the fat," exposing the muscle and bone of the organization. Conflict, chaos, and disillusionment are often the result. Employees have been urged to do more, been expected to make sacrifices, and have been praised for being strong team members, only to see another round of layoffs and reorganization. As frustration and resentment mount, this is where we have seen disgruntled employees show up with guns and shoot up workplaces.

Of course, that is the most violent and tragic expression of the damage toxicity can cause. Some of the other factors contributing to toxicity are systemic. For example, it has been reported that nearly one in five American workers were subjected to some form of verbal abuse, unwanted sexual attention, threats, humiliating behavior, physical violence, bullying, harassment, or sexual harassment at work in the past year.⁵ This translates to about **17 percent** of American workers.

Too often, bullying is evident in toxic leaders whose aggressive, mean-spirited, and disrespectful actions are tolerated or even rewarded. Behaviors that cause employees to experience regular physical symptoms of stress, frustration, and depression are not limited to lower-level employees. These same symptoms can manifest in leaders at all levels of management. Until companies find ways of genuinely valuing all employees, they will not benefit from the long-term value of a stable and secure workforce at every level within the organization. Survey after survey reinforces the fact that people want job security, but not at any cost.

Smart organizations that anticipate the future of work start by striving to attain the hallmark indicators that employees, especially the young and talented, are demanding. To build a healthy, non-toxic culture with non-toxic leaders capable of attracting top talent and keeping your legal department out of court, coordinated efforts should start at the top—with the CEO and their leadership team modeling healthy behavior and not tolerating anything less in the organization. As we see in the foregoing

---

⁵ https://www.rand.org/blog/2017/08/many-americans-face-bullying-harrassment-and-abuse.html

list of companies' workers who don't want to leave, strong, trustworthy, decisive leadership has a direct impact on talent retention.

Building a healthy workplace provides the most durable foundation for employee retention and productivity. Here are some essential actions and best practices business leaders can take to promote a desirable culture.

1. **Define toxic behavior:** The executive-leadership team has to start with a clear definition of what form toxic behaviors take in their workplace, while recognizing the cost tolerating toxicity extracts from their organization. Soliciting feedback from employees is an important first step toward articulating an effective working definition of what their norms and expectations are. One useful tool for gathering information is an annual employee-engagement survey. To derive the most benefit from the survey, the process should be promoted as important and actionable. Too often in toxic cultures, the subsequent report presents the results in a manner designed solely to make the organization look good. High-scoring areas are highlighted, and some "safe" areas are chosen for improvement. Toxic organizations allow toxic leaders to use manipulated survey data as a weapon to justify their leadership styles rather than as an opportunity for development.

   The executive-leadership team should use the data honestly and share the results transparently to identify elements of existing toxicity and to shape a process for moving toward a non-toxic culture. Employees should be made aware that the new cultural norms leaders set forth reflect the feedback they provided. The executive-leadership team must draw clear lines of zero tolerance for behaviors identified as contributing to toxicity. Any new policies and procedures should be openly shared with the entire organization, consistently enforced and regularly measured for compliance.

2. **Establish leadership performance goals:** To get the attention of leadership and bring about new organizational behaviors, engaging their wallets is a time-honored tactic. Most organizations' "pay for performance" policies tie directly to measurable metrics and/or the results of performance goals. After the executive-leadership team determines what behaviors will have zero tolerance in the organization, each leader has to be held accountable for meeting the expectation. Failure to comply should come with a heavy cost in their performance evaluation as a tangible indication of the value the organization places on eliminating toxic behaviors.

3. **Set key policies and procedures:** Real change is most likely to succeed if and when the executive-leadership team serves as role models, sponsors, and promoters of all company policies strengthening a healthy work culture. Certain policies have proven effective, such as a true "open door" reporting policy, empowering employees at all levels to safely take their concerns up one or more levels and reporting them to upper management. Many organizations believe they have such a practice in place. However, all too often, they may have the policy, but these conversations are not monitored or acted upon. Consequently, the toxic leader, uncensored, returns to their aggressive behaviors. Organizational policies and procedures are the enforceable laws of the company. They are designed to protect both the employee and the company. When companies can demonstrate that they police and enforce their own policies fairly and consistently, employees gain trust in the organization and the leadership.

4. **Dismantle enabler behavior:** Organizations that build, monitor, and enforce non-toxic culture from the C suite down should empower lower-level leaders and employees not only to recognize and report toxic behaviors but to identify enablers of toxic

leadership. Toxic leaders with diagnosable personality disorders frequently maintain their power by surrounding themselves with followers. These "enablers" explicitly or implicitly condone the toxic leader's behaviors by covering it up, finding ways to excuse it, or even celebrating the so-called "effectiveness" of the toxic leader. They refuse to acknowledge the damage the leader's behavior wreaks on their co-workers or its negative impact on the organizational culture. The destructive aspect of toxic leaders is not their work performance in terms of company product. It is the number of bodies they trample on to achieve their high performance. Enablers who are peers of the toxic leader form a protective shield within the organization at their level of management.

There are a number of factors that can give rise to enablers. Some may feel unable to criticize the toxic leader because they are convinced that senior leadership holds the toxic performer in high regard, that the abusive boss is "untouchable." Others may fear that objecting to the toxic leader's tactics would be career suicide. Still others may believe their blind loyalty will be rewarded.

Numerous business scandals and politically motivated events offer painful examples of people acting as enablers to toxic leaders. Deceptive, illegal leadership practices led thousands of employees at Theranos, FTX, WeWork, Volkswagen, Wells Fargo, and other once-respected organizations to go against their better judgment to follow dictates of bad behaviors. The real threat of losing their good jobs compelled them to choose to overlook, ignore, or justify the toxic leader's directives and actions.

In the increasingly polarized environment of American politics, we see numerous examples of enabler behavior playing out in support of proponents of political extremes. Staff, appointees, funders, and party loyalists find themselves constantly justifying, rationalizing, or apologizing for the outrageous behaviors of public figures exhibiting diagnosable personality disorders. Being caught up in an enabling role may lead otherwise decent people to break the law or cross other boundaries of civility that previously would have been unthinkable to them. The longer enablers "go along to get along," the more difficult it becomes to admit that things have gone too far. Healthy workplaces encourage and support respectful questioning of authority or judgment. Employees who feel they have permission to challenge what may seem like unfair or ill-conceived decisions can play a vital role in moderating or defusing potentially toxic leadership behavior. Work cultures that allow employees to voice their grievances without fear of punishment are more likely to be environments in which workers and management jointly arrive at the best practices and policies that promote greater productivity and positivity.

If the work culture prohibits all challenges to authority or decisions, employees are left with far fewer options. Unhappy, discouraged, or frustrated talent may decide their only choice is to resign or, in extreme cases, may feel they need to make the courageous move from enabler to whistleblower.

5. **Require leadership training:** Diagnosable personality disorders play a major role in establishing and perpetuating a toxic culture. Organizations that design leadership-training curricula to include rigorous assessment components can often identify many of these toxic behaviors before they derail the organization. Properly constructed, professionally administered leadership training should begin well before any employee receives their first leadership assignment. Making training and assessment a prerequisite for high-potential employees prior to their first assignment will enable early detection of possible personality issues. At this early stage, intervention may be able to modify

the individual's approach to leadership before they are entrusted with any significant authority.

Organizations that provide the proper mental-health support and leadership training are more likely to attract and retain top talent. Well-designed leadership-development curricula should be directed at and required for all levels of leadership: frontline, middle management, senior-level leadership, and even executive C-suite level. Integrating training and targeted personal coaching into the formal process of professional development shows the value an organization places on the desire employees have for continuous growth and improvement. Making this commitment is more proof of a company culture in which employees are valued.

6. **Build meaningful, enforceable diversity, equity, and inclusion (DEI) policies**

Millennials and Gen Z, who are the future of the workforce, are increasingly holding companies accountable for the claims they make about their organization's commitment to principles and practices actively promoting diversity, equity, and inclusion. Boasting about DEI claims in corporate advertisements and during big town-hall speeches to employees falls far short of their expectations. It is no longer enough for a company to offer well-publicized DEI programs during Black History Month or Pride Week. Employees expect to see a genuine commitment to DEI reflected in enforceable organizational policies and procedures, starting with, but going beyond, recruiting, hiring practices, and career advancement.

Employees expect DEI practices to support the development of *all* employees, not just the chosen few who traditionally look and sound like upper-level leadership. Younger employees, in particular, want active affinity groups and time to participate in these groups without fear of negative performance impact. Many younger workers are choosing their employers based on the expectation that, as employees, they will be able to be their "authentic self." They do not expect to be required to disguise their identity or sacrifice their overall well-being in order to be successful in their professional position. In a 2021 survey by LinkedIn Talent Solutions, one in four job seekers stated that DEI is the *most important area* of investment organizations can make to improve company culture.

Risha Grant, an award-winning DEI speaker and expert, brings this message to corporate leaders: "A strong DE&I presence creates a culture where employees feel empowered to be authentic and bring new ideas based on their unique knowledge and experiences. . . . You will not have a good company culture if DE&I is not present."**

As leaders consider their organization's future and seek to engage the most talented and highly desirable employees, DEI should be a major component of their overall strategy. Well-conceived, consistently executed DEI policies and practices improve the workplace for everyone. And a healthy corporate culture ultimately enhances the overall productivity and economic viability of every organization.

7. **Create trust through transparency**

Organizational trust is an essential cornerstone supporting employee engagement. And employee engagement is the main ingredient for high levels of productivity. Every business and nonprofit enterprise strives for maximum productivity, since high productivity often leads to success. Yet leaders who create, promote, or tolerate toxic environments are, in effect, destroying

---

** https://www.shrm.org/resourcesandtools/hr-topics/behavioral-competencies/global-and-cultural-effectiveness/pages/the-relationship-between-culture-and-dei.aspx

trust. Once trust begins to erode, a powerful poison can spread quickly through your organization, with devastating effects. Toxic organizations lack trust, and, as a consequence, they often suffer dual impacts—the loss of talented, tenured employees and the constriction of a pipeline for hiring new top talent.

Organizations can avoid such damage to their hiring prospects and ensure employee retention by working to eliminate the range of classic toxic behaviors described throughout earlier chapters. Efforts to root out toxicity should begin with a commitment to genuine transparency. All employees should see their managers not just speaking out against toxic behavior but leading by example. One of the most valuable areas of transparency involves clarity about strategy and potential impending changes to organizational structure. After decades of sudden and catastrophic layoffs and "right sizing" by businesses in a wide variety of industries, employees have become wary of signing on to companies with a history of unanticipated workforce reductions intended to increase returns for investors. Where once a company may have been the top choice for high-performing talent, employees report downgrading some formerly desirable employers to second or third choice because of a perceived lack of job security.

Top employees recognize that there are going to be unplanned and uncontrollable disruptions to the marketplace that require organizations to adapt. They do not expect that change will never occur. What they do expect and increasingly demand is transparency about organizational changes that impact their jobs. Even when changes are less dramatic than layoffs or terminations, employees look for honest communication from their managers and leaders. They want respect and fair consideration that recognizes the tremendous impact of proposed changes on themselves and their families. Clear and transparent communication provides opportunities for employees to make informed decisions about whether they will continue working for the company or move on. Hard decisions still have to be made, but trust can be preserved.

In my consulting practice, employees have repeatedly expressed their disillusionment with toxic managers who willfully continue to promote strategy Y despite knowing that strategy X will soon replace it, eliminating jobs and derailing careers. The employees who survive the cuts no longer have faith in their own future with the company. Often even the survivors of some forms of management deception find ways to retaliate. These may take the form of work slowdowns, product or service "sabotage," class-action lawsuits, or social-media attacks. We have all read accounts of what can happen with disgruntled former employees—violent physical attacks directed at toxic managers and other innocent organizational employees. I believe that, by rooting out toxic and misguided leadership practices, widespread dissatisfaction, disillusionment, and related workplace tragedy can be averted.

Visionary leaders at every level within their organization must recognize that *every conversation and every interaction a manager has with an employee affects their level of engagement*. Research indicates that fully engaged employees are 38 percent more productive than disengaged employees. (A more detailed source would suggest highly engaged employees are 38% more likely to have above-average productivity.[††]

As a leader, your ability to capture that level of engagement can be the differentiator between your company and your closest competitors. Smart, successful organizations have learned that reducing or eliminating toxicity by building trust through transparency results in a stronger, healthier organization.

[††] https://enliten.net/dev/wp-content/uploads/2018/06/Employee-Engagement-1-Statistics-17-11-01.pdf)

INTERVENTIONS MAKE ALL THE DIFFERENCE

Over many years of professional practice, I have advised and supported leaders confronted by uncertainty over how to manage individuals whose diagnosable personality disorders and subsequent toxic behaviors were severely damaging their organizations. My experience proves that, when toxic behavior is not tolerated or excused by the "top of the house," organizations begin to see a successful, healthy remediation of work culture.

In the next few sections, I've offered short case studies that describe the circumstances leading up to three of the most common outcomes after interventions. These are dismissal, demotion, and successful re-integration.

Ultimately, it is up to the person with the diagnosable personality disorder to choose their response to a professional intervention and remediation plan. No one can compel the toxic leader to change their damaging ways. However, two consistent facts characterize my years of professional consulting. If senior management does nothing to curtail the behavior of a toxic leader, the entire organization will continue to suffer, especially in the areas of talent acquisition and retention. Secondly, the earlier an intervention occurs, the more likely the cost of irreparable organizational damage and the pain of termination can be avoided. Don't wait. The problems caused by a leader with diagnosable personality disorders will never simply disappear.

a. **Too little, too late is an unwelcome reality**

In many cases a good organizational consultant can be extremely effective at diagnosing the most critical root cause of the team's dysfunctions, creating and executing an effective OD solution. However, in cases where the toxicity has been tolerated for a long time, or in situations where the toxic leader's diagnosable personal disorder is too severe to be treated, the only possible outcome may be the most extreme: termination of the employee.

Unfortunately, this was the case with Dr. Douglas Thomas, lead scientist at a large pharma company. The impact of his narcissistic behavior on his team had reached a level sufficient to derail their work on the company's blockbuster drug for a rare form of children's cancer. Dr. Thomas was reported to have been nasty, condescending, and insulting to the other professionals on the team. He believed himself to be so superior in scientific knowledge and skill that he questioned why certain others were even allowed to work on such an important project. Dr. Thomas publicly and repeatedly took credit for all the team's achievements, causing deep embarrassment and resentment among the team, especially since most of them were as accomplished, if not more notable, than Dr. Thomas.

Although many seasoned scientists and commercial business professionals on Dr. Thomas's team had made serious complaints about his toxic behavior, senior management had, so far, taken no action. As a result of Dr. Thomas's narcissistic toxic leadership, team members asked to transfer out of the unit, and many were threatening to quit the company altogether.

After finally heeding the team's warnings, the executive vice president of the rare disease business division hired a consultant to conduct an assessment of the team. This study revealed the extent of the serious damage Dr. Thomas's behavior was inflicting on the team and the company culture. An organizational intervention was proposed, beginning with an alignment conversation between his supervisor and Dr. Thomas.

Contrary to the hopes of senior management, the extent of Dr. Thomas's narcissistic disorder prevented him from acknowledging that there were any flaws in his leadership style. He refused to accept any responsibility for the low morale and many defections of the top professionals on his team. Instead, he insisted that the EVP direct his attention to retraining members of the project team or replacing any disgruntled employees with new team members.

Without a willingness to accept responsibility or be open to any behavior modification, it was clear there could be no alignment between the EVP and Dr. Thomas regarding project goals, team norms, or organizational values. The EVP was left with no choice but to sever Dr. Thomas from the organization. The outcome may have been different had senior management not tolerated, excused, or even rewarded Dr. Thomas's toxic leadership for so long. Years of senior management's avoidance of the problem allowed Dr. Thomas to feel his abusive style was validated by the success of his team. In fact, he had caused extensive damage to the highly skilled workforce and the company culture. Termination was the only avenue left to senior management to stop the impact of his toxic behavior.

b. Demotion can limit the damage

One option for a successful outcome of an Occupational Development intervention is to retain the highly talented leader conditionally by reassigning them to a lower level of responsibility. This may prove to be a temporary situation, enabling the employee to demonstrate both their willingness and ability to correct the diagnosable personality disorders contributing to their toxic behavior.

Serena Hollins was the senior director for a digital learning organization in a large nonprofit institution. Unfortunately, her borderline personality created a powerfully toxic work environment. Serena's unpredictable, unstable behavior created confusion for her leadership team, resulting in frustration, anxiety, and overall job dissatisfaction, all of which severely hampered their productivity. Fear of incurring the legendary "wrath of Serena" made the team reluctant to make even simple leadership decisions. Instead, they felt they had no choice but to constantly defer everything to Serena.

Some days Serena was full of confidence and engaged with all of the members of her leadership team. On other days, she would make remarks that caused interpersonal conflict with team members, even at times forcing team members to choose sides—not about work issues but around loyalty to her vs. other team members. Serena bragged to her team about how she managed her stressful days with an overabundance of "dark brown liquor." Her impulsive, dramatic, unpredictable but frequent mood swings kept the team off balance. Her management style ranged from extreme micromanagement to near-total avoidance and isolation, even going so far as to suddenly work from home or stay in her office with the door closed all day, canceling or rescheduling all of her appointments. These swings could fluctuate from day to day or even from morning to afternoon.

After noticing a significant decline in the team's performance, Serena's senior leader met with her to discuss how Serena was showing up to her team. Although these conversations are never easy, Serena was willing to admit she felt overwhelmed in her current leadership role. With her supervisor's support, Serena agreed to seek help that would enable her to change her behavior. Serena was removed as team leader and assigned to special projects without supervisory responsibilities. During this time, she was required to attend leadership-development training and work one on one with an organizational-leadership coach.

The combination of a supportive senior leader, professional coaching, and, most importantly, a genuine desire to change brought about a win for both the organization and Serena. The organization was able to retain a very talented colleague, and Serena was able to demonstrate that she was capable of positive change, putting her on track for a productive future with her company.

c. **Intervention and reintegration**

Earlier, we saw an example of a head nurse with a diagnosable unstable personality disorder who bullied and belittled her team of more than 200 nurses. Over time, senior leadership came to realize that, even though her bullying management style may have saved the organization thousands of dollars in audit fines, her toxic behavior was costing them far more in staff morale, engagement, and the ability to retain top talent. The leadership team made a commitment to stop enabling or ignoring her destructive behaviors. The executive director contracted with an organizational-development professional to devise a program to turn around a damaging situation.

A key part of the proposed interventions required the bullying nurse to participate in leadership assessments, coaching, and retraining both as an individual and as part of peer cohorts. The assessments brought her to a shocking realization of how negatively she was showing up as a leader. Over an eight- to twelve-month period of time, as a direct result of intervention and training, this leader's behavior began to change. The number of anonymous complaints being sent to the regional and national office went from ten to twelve per month to an amazing *zero*. Staff reported that they were learning from this very talented nurse leader, and work was actually fun again.

CONCLUSION

Generally, all employees—even the toxic leader—come to work with the goal of doing a good job.

In most cases, leaders don't intend to be toxic or create a toxic culture. My years of working with leaders and organizations have revealed one or more of these four issues as the basis for toxic leadership:

1. The leader lacks awareness of how they are showing up to the team or organization and the negative impact they have on team productivity, team members' job satisfaction, and level of engagement.

2. The toxic leader may be exhibiting a diagnosable personality disorder that can be managed effectively with treatment, training, or both.

3. In many cases, toxic leaders have never been given the proper training to enable them to become good leaders. Lacking the skills, knowledge, and preparation to effectively lead a team, they too often resort to imitating other toxic leaders they feel have been rewarded by the organization.

4. Organizations must be careful to avoid creating a toxic culture based on a lack of trust, or on unreasonable demands by asking employees to "make bricks without straw." When senior leaders promote a culture of suspicion and unrealistic expectations, middle managers feel they must perpetuate this type of environment in order to earn promotions. In this way, toxic leadership permeates an entire organization.

The purpose of this book is to point out the serious impact that a toxic leader or toxic culture can have on the overall health of your team or business, especially when the toxic leader has a diagnosable personality disorder. To help you recognize what may underlie the real-life situations you're experiencing in your workplace, I've shared case studies from my consulting practice. These case studies provide insights for dealing with toxic leaders and suggest who should be involved to support your efforts.

When an organization's senior leadership is committed to addressing toxic management practices, often they will engage a professional to work with the leader, team, or organization. Effective management may require intervention by trained professionals to help you achieve transformational resolution. In most cases, these situations can be resolved with professional assistance, restoring the company culture through healthy win-win resolutions.

A strong partnership among senior leadership, human-resource client partners, and learning-and-development professionals is essential in bringing about positive cultural change. Organizations that are truly committed to creating a healthy company culture make significant physical and financial investments in building and maintaining this partnership. This investment makes possible a proactive approach to identifying and addressing emerging toxic behaviors before the damage occurs.

Only a sincere commitment to helping a toxic leader improve how they show up, how they engage their co-workers, and how they impact the organizational outcomes will be effective. With this sort of partnership in place, we tend to see strong alignment between the toxic leader and the organization in terms of a willingness to bring about necessary change. For the toxic leader with a diagnosable personality disorder, this could mean committing to coaching, training, and possibly to regular clinical treatment (e.g., medication, psychotherapy, support groups such as Alcoholics Anonymous, etc.)

My work has shown that, regardless of the cause, toxic leaders and toxic cultures can be transformed into healthy leaders capable of managing positive work environments. The solutions that have proven to be most effective are holistic and systematic, and they emanate from the top of the organization. The goal for truly visionary leadership must be to foster a culture enabling all employees to work, learn, and grow and to create a healthy organization, one that retains top talent and ultimately thrives.

For all of us whose role is protecting the welfare of workers, it is worth remembering that *all employees come to work with the goal of doing a good job.* Our most important responsibility is to do everything we can to help them reach that goal.

Sources

"Ramani Durvasula, PhD, (February 20, 2024) It's Not You: Identifying and Healing from Narcissistic People, The Open Field"

"Barlow, Don, (April 1, 2021) Gaslighting & Narcissistic Abuse Recovery: Recover from Emotional Abuse, Recognize Narcissists & Manipulators and Break Free Once and for All"

"Covey, Stephen M.R., with Kasperson, David, Covey, McKinkee, Judd, Gary T., (April 5, 2022) Trust and Inspire: How Truly Great Leaders Unleash Greatness in Others, Simon & Schuster,"

"Peter Block, (January 1, 2011) Flawless Consulting: A Guide to Getting Your Expertise Used, Third Edition, Pfeiffer & Co"

"American Psychiatric Association, (March 16, 2022) Diagnostic and Statistical Manual of Mental Disorders, Text Revision Dsm-5-tr 5th Edition, Amer Psychiatric Pub Inc"

"Warrenfeltz, Rodney, Kellett, Trish (November 14, 2016) Coaching the Dark Side of Personality, Hogan Press"

"Abigail Phillips (January 17, 2017) Toxic bosses in the workplace, The University of Manchester Alliance Manchester Business School"

"Raj Subrameyer (October 6, 2021) The Three Symptoms of Toxic Leadership and How to Get out of It, InfoQ"

"Alan Goldman, (November 8, 2006) Goldman, A. (2006). High toxicity leadership: Borderline personality disorder and the dysfunctional organization. Journal of Managerial Psychology"

"Indeed Editoral, (July 1, 2024)Toxic Leadership (With Definition and a List of Traits)"

"Matt Higgins, (March 28, 2023) A CEO shares the 5 toxic personality types he sees 'over and over' again—'I stay far away'"

"Tim Minahan, (May 31, 2021) What Your Future Employees Want Most, Harvard Business Review"

"Ed O'Boyle, (March 30, 2021) 4 Things GenZ and Millennial Expect From Their Workplace, Gallup"

"Punneet Sandhu, (January 24, 2023) 9 Sign Youre in a Toxic Work Environment and What to Do About It"

"Deep Patel (March 27 2017) 10 Signs You're A Terrrible Leader, Forbes"

"Sam Campbell (September 19, 2023) 9 Ways To Fix A Toxic Work Environment, When I Work Blog"

"Rob Asghar (September 16, 2014) How Toxic Followers Enable Toxic Leaders, Forbes"

"Raj Subrameyer (April 13, 2022) Leadership and How to Get out of It, Toxic Leadership and its Impact"

"Borderline Personality Disoder, Mayo Foundation for Medical Education and Research"

"Heidi Lynne Kurter (December 23, 2019) 4 Strategies To Repair A Toxic Culture From The Top Down, Forbes"

"Theo Veldsman (January 13, 2016) How toxic leaders destroy people as well as organisations, The Conversation"

"Linda Too, Michael Harvey (2012) "'Toxic'" workplaces: the negative interface between the physical and social environment, Emerald Group Publishing Limited"

"McKinsey& Company. (June 2020) Understand organizational barriers to a more inclusive workplace, Jorg Gre"

"Elisabeth Egan (March 29, 2024) How to Deal with a Narcissist, The New York Times"

"Ron Carucci (January 24, 2028) How to Deal with a Passive-Aggressive Boss, Harvard Business Review"

"Amy Cooper Hakim (January 8, 2017) When Your Boss Is a Narcissist, Psychology Today"

"Rebecca Knight (April 1, 2016) How to Work for a Narcissistic Boss, Harvard Business Review"

Sources

"Karol M. Wasylyhyn, Hal S. Shorey and Jason S Chaffin (December 2012) Patterns of Leadership Behaviour: Implications for Successful Executive Coaching Outcomes, The British Psychological Society"

"Larry Hughes, (January 18, 2021) Challenging Goliath: Leadership Lessons from the Life of King David,"

"Lindsey Joyce Chamberlain, Randy Hodson (20210) Toxic Work environments: What Helps and What Hurts, Sociological Perspectives"

"Jeff Doolittle (2023) Life-Changing Leadership Habits, Organizational Talent Consulting"

"John C. Maxwell (2019) Leader Shift, Harper Collins Leadership"

"James Kouzes, Barry Posner (2012) The leadership Challenge 5th ed. Published by The Leadership Challenge (A Wiley Brand)"

Acknowledgments

"The master in the art of living makes little distinction between his work and his play, his labor and his leisure, his mind and his body, his information and his recreation, his love and his religion. He hardly knows which is which. He simply pursues his vision of excellence at whatever he does, leaving others to decide whether he is working or playing. To him, he's always doing both."

By James Michener

WRITING A BOOK WAS HARDER than I thought, but clearly more rewarding than I could have envisioned. None of this would be possible without my belief in my favorite scripture, Philippians 4:13, "I can do all things through Christ who gives me strength." My Pastor, Dr. Addis Moore, a great leader himself, has trained me to create a faith statement, connecting my understanding of the scriptures to what I believe. I had never written a book before, so leaning on my own understanding was not an option. Beyond my spiritual belief, there are many individuals I need to acknowledge who supported and encouraged me in one way or another during this project.

While I included my wife, Dr. Toni Woolfork-Barnes, in the dedication, I feel it is important to recognize the many roles she plays in my life that impact my focus and drive. A consummate professional in her own career, she still finds time to be a thought partner, motivator, coach, counselor, advisor, mother, best friend, and proofreader. We would not be here without you; I love you.

I am extremely grateful to Dr. Larry Irey, my mentor and one of the most talented psychologists I know, for the many years of clinical training regarding personality disorders. Everyone needs a Larry in their life.

Dr. Carla Adkison-Johnson, the author of "Child Discipline in African American Families: Culturally Responsive Policies," helped me with the literature search and key research that shaped this project. Thanks, Carla. She, along with her husband, Dr. Phillip D. Johnson, who is my fraternity brother, provided unconditional support, friendship, and encouragement to keep going on this project. Phil would say, "Keep writing, we need this book"; thanks, Nupe.

I want to thank some key leaders in my career who motivated me and modeled good leadership. These were leaders who provided training, feedback, opportunities, transparency, and trust. They coached me, ensured I had the tools needed for success, and took pride in my achievements. I sincerely want to acknowledge and thank Kevin Munson, Steve Kontra, Tanya Clemens, and Sun Sun Chung.

I am sincerely appreciative that Dr. Jeff Doolittle, the author of "Life-Changing Leadership Habits," always answered the phone when I called with questions. He shared his experience as an author and encouraged me as a friend. Wow!

With extreme gratitude, I acknowledge friends who read sections of my manuscript, served as thought partners, or shared their experiences as authors throughout the project. Special thanks go to Dr. Rita Jump, Dr. Larry Hughes, Dr. Taylor Sherman, and Dr. Evelyn Winfield-Thomas. Special thanks to Robyn Hughes graphic designer extraordinaire, for her input on the front cover design.

Thank you to all the human resource professionals who allowed me to interview them or share toxic cases from their careers, such as

Acknowledgments

Steve Manley, Danni Hill, Angela Daniels, and Robyn Davis, just to name a few.

Family is incredibly important to me, and I want to acknowledge the impact these individuals have had on my life. With much love and respect, I thank uncles T, Milton, and Ed, as well as aunts Katherine, Annette, Jeanette, Betty, Lenora, Donna, Diana, Jackie, Harriet, Kenneth, and a host of cousins. These family members have all embraced the importance of family support and have been taught to "get up and at it every day. We are never out worked." Finally, I want to acknowledge a couple of close friends, Isaac Lockhart and Dr. Gerri Browning.

About the Author

DR. OLLIE G. BARNES III is a trusted organizational performance consultant and the founder of Impact Performance Consultants (IPC). With over 25 years of experience, he has collaborated with global Fortune 500 companies to transform leadership and enhance team dynamics. Known for his creative, behavior-based solutions to complex organizational challenges, Dr. Barnes excels in developing interactive learning solutions that build employee capabilities with significant results.

Dr. Barnes brings a unique blend of clinical and organizational expertise, driven by a passion for applying psychology to help entire organizations thrive. Rather than focusing solely on individual clients, he treats the organization itself as the patient, aiming to improve its overall health and effectiveness.

Before founding IPC, Dr. Barnes served as a senior leader in Global Learning and Development at Pfizer Inc., where he honed his skills in leadership and organizational development. Trained in both clinical and organizational psychology he adopts a comprehensive approach when coaching and resolving organizational and human resource issues.

Throughout his career, Dr. Barnes has positively impacted employees in over 170 markets across North America, Latin America, Asia Pacific, Europe, and the Middle East. His dedication to enhancing organizational effectiveness through leadership development and employee engagement has made him a trusted advisor to many companies worldwide. Known for his innovative methods and proven success, Dr. Barnes is an expert in the field of organizational learning and employee performance.

Index

A

absenteeism, 94–96
accountability, leadership and, 35
Action Planning phase of project, 133
addictive behaviors, BPD and, 60–61
alliances in consulting position, 118
ambiguity issues, 140
AMP (Attachment Motivation Performance) assessment, 121, 123
antisocial personality disorder, 136
autonomy, leadership and, 35
avoidant personality disorder, 137

B

Bartell, Rod, 121
bench strength, 91–92
best practices
    DEI policies, 167–168
    leadership performance goals, 164
    leadership training, 166–167
    policies and procedures, 164
    toxic behavior, defining, 163
    toxic enablers, dismantling, 164–165
    transparency, 168–170
    trust, 168–170
blame
    shifting, passive-aggressive leaders, 51
    BPD and, 59–60
    passive-aggressive leaders, 47
BPD (borderline personality disorder), 59, 136
    addictive behaviors, 60–61, 79–80, 81
    blame and, 59–60
    communications chaos, 66–67, 80–81

dividing teams, 81–82

extreme physical situations, 63

gender and, 60–61

image saving, 72–73

inappropriate physical contact, 68, 79

outrage when questioned, 76, 80–81

self-harm, 61

termination reaction, 64–66

toxic enablers, 83

burnout, 100–101

C

case studies

BPD leader, 62–66, 68–77, 78–84

narcissistic leaders, 3–9, 10–12, 13–17

passive-aggressive leader, 40–55

CHRO (chief human resources officer), 3

closure meeting, 147

communication

BPD chaos, 66–67

leadership and, 35

passive-aggressive leaders, 40

company role, shift in, 151–152

compliance person, 147

consultants, 112

benefits, 114–115

D

decision making, 96–97

DEI (diversity, equity, and inclusion), 156–157

demotion, 173–174

dependent personality disorder, 137

diagnosis, process, 107–109

Diagnostic and Statistical Manual of Mental Disorders (DSM). See DSM

Diagnostic phase of project, 116–117

discovery, 121–126

Hogan Assessment, 124–125

interviews

group-level assessment, 126–129

sample questions, 129–132

team-level assessment, 126–129

methods, 121–126

Myers-Briggs assessment, 126

difficult-conversation methods, narcissistic leaders, 26–27

DSM (The Diagnostic and Statistical Manual of Mental Disorders) IV, 112–114

DSM-5-TR

Cluster A, 135–136

Cluster B, 136–137

Cluster C, 137–138

passive-aggressive personality disorder, 134–135

E

ecology of workplace, 157–158

ego-syntonic, 20

employee health issues, 94–96, 162

enabling behaviors, xiii

Entry phase of project, 116

alliances in position, 118

contract building, 120–121

engagement, agreeing to, 119

power, 118
project expertise, 120
ethics, Gen Z and Millennials, 154–155
EVP, 172–173

F
findings, 142–145
  candor, 142
  closure meeting, 147
  HIPAA and, 143
  private meetings, 142–143
  responses, 143
  Team Charter, 144–145
  team meeting, 143–144
FTX, 165

G
gaslighting, 128–129
GCM (global commercial marketing) unit, 3
Gen Z workers, company culture and, 152–159
generations by birth period, 153
group-level assessments, 126–129

H
he said/she said situations, passive-aggressive leader, 51–52
health issues of employees, 94–96, 162
health of workplace, improving, 161–170
HIPAA (Health Insurance Portability and Accountability Act), 143
HiPo (high-potential), 3

toxic leader impact, 91–92
hiring process two-way street, 152
histrionic personality disorder, 136–137
Hogan, Joyce, 38
Hogan, Robert, 38
Hogan Assessment, 38, 43, 124–125

I
Implementation phase of project, 140–142
impression management, 43–44
inadequacy, feelings of, passive-aggressive leaders, 47
individualized respect in the workplace, 157
insight, 20
institutional wisdom, xii
intervention, 117, 171–175
  demotion, 173–174
  reintegration, 174–175
interviews (during project), 99
  Action planning phase, 138–139
  contract design and, 120
  exit interviews, 89, 111
  Diagnostic phase, 126–129
    sample questions, 129–132
  impression management, 43–44
Isaacson, Walter *(Steve Jobs)*, 34
isolation, 35

J
Jobs, Steve, 34

L
lateral moves, 3

leadership
  accountability, 35
  autonomy, 35
  communication, 35
  development programs, 157
  normal conditions, 140–141
  under pressure, 140–141
  qualifications, 140
  trust, 35
learning programs, 157
Leisurely personality type (Hogan
  Assessment), 38, 43

M

managers, passive-aggressive leader
  interactions, 44–45
micro-aggressions, passive-aggressive
  leaders, 36
Millennial workers, company culture
  and, 152–159
morale, 99–100
Myers-Briggs assessment, 126

N

narcissism
  BPD and, 60
  term origins, 21
narcissistic leaders. *See also* toxic
  leaders
  challenges, 20–21
  characteristics, 17–20
  difficult-conversation methods,
    26–27
  documentation, 26
  enabling behaviors, avoiding, 26

  engaging, 28–29
  identifying behavior, 24–25
  influencing, 27–28
  insights, 20
  interactions, 22–22
  positivity of, 29–30
  proactive conversations, 25–26
  questioning oneself, 27
  rage, 26–27
  retaliation, 26–27
  role-playing interactions, 29
  Trump, Donald, 33
narcissistic personality disorder, 137
Narcissus, 21

O

obsessive-compulsive disorder (OCD),
  137–138
obsessive-compulsive personality disorder (OCPD), 137–138
ODDIS (Organizational Diagnostic
  and Development System),
  121–123
organizational impact, 87
  absenteeism, 94–96
  burnout, 100–101
  decision making, 96–97
  employee health, 94–96
  hiring and, 90–91
  morale, 99–100
  offer acceptance, 90
  productivity, 97–99
  promotions, 91–94
  recruitment and, 90–91
  retention rates, 88–89

trust, 101–102
unethical behavior, 102–103

P
paranoid personality disorder, 135
passive-aggressive leaders
blame shifting, 51
blamelessness, 47
communication, 40
control and, 48
direct report interactions, 44–49
dismissing "underlings," 45
DSM-5-TR inclusion, 134–135
he said/she said situations, 51–52
Hogan Assessment, 38
identifying, 38–40
inadequacy, feelings of, 47
inconsistencies, 45
manager interactions, 44–45
micro-aggressions, 36
one-on-one meetings, 48
reactions to questioning, 36–37
root causes, 38–39
toxic enablers, 39
converting, 52
"Who's on First?" analogy, 37
personality disorders
indicators, 128, 134–135
toxic leader link, 134–139
political sphere, 165–166
power in organization, 118
productivity, 97–99
project phases, 115
Action Planning, 133
Diagnostic, 116–117, 121–132

Entry, 116, 117–121
Implementation, 140–142
Termination, 146–148
promises, passive-aggressive leader, 44
promotions, 91–94

R
retention rates, 88–89
companies with high rates, 159–161
ROI (return on investment), AMP
and, 123
role-playing interactions, narcissistic
leaders, 29

S
schizoid personality disorder, 135–136
schizotypal personality disorder, 136
secrecy, 35
self-harm, BPD and, 61
self-protection in toxic leaders, 117
shift in company role, 151–152
solution, 117
Steve Jobs (Isaacson), 34
sustainability plan, 148

T
talent retention, AMP and, 123
Team Charter, 144–145
team-level assessments, 126–129
Termination phase of project, 146
closure meeting, 147
compliance person, 147
contract and, 146
sustainability plan, 148
Theranos, 165

toxic enablers, 34
  BPD (borderline personality dis-
    order), 83
  dismantling the behavior, 164–165
  passive-aggressive leaders, 39
    converting to, 52
toxic leaders
  basis for toxic leadership, 175–177
  contributing factors, 140–142
  Jobs, Steve, 34
  personality disorder link, 134–139
  results and, 34
  self-protection, 117
  terminology, 107
  toxic enablers, 34
  versus toxic organizations, 141–142
toxic organizations, 141–142
transparency, Millennials and, 155–156
Trump, Donald, 33
trust, leadership and, 35
  organizational impact, 101–102

V
Volkswagen, 165

W–Z
Watch Outs, 114–115
well-being, elements of, 154
Wells Fargo, 165
WeWork, 165
Whicker, Marci Lynn, 107
"Who's on First?" analogy of passive-
    aggressive leaders, 37
workplace health improvements,
    161–170

www.ingramcontent.com/pod-product-compliance
Lightning Source LLC
Chambersburg PA
CBHW071601210326
41597CB00019B/3348